Advertising Annual 2002

Advertising Annual 2002

The International Annual of Advertising
Das internationale Jahrbuch der Werbung
La référence internationale de la publicité

CEO & Creative Director: B. Martin Pedersen

Publisher: Doug Wolske
Publications Director: Michael Gerbino

Editors: Andrea Birnbaum, Michael Porciello
and Heinke Jenssen

Art Director: Lauren Slutsky
Design & Production: Joseph Liotta
and Nicole Recchia

Published by Graphis Inc.

Contents Inhalt Sommaire

Remarks: We extend our heartfelt thanks to contributors throughout the world who have made it possible to publish a wide and international spectrum of the best work in this field. Entry instructions for all Graphis Books may be requested from: **Graphis Inc.**, 307 Fifth Avenue, Tenth Floor, New York, NY 10016, or visit our Web site at www.graphis.com.

Anmerkungen: Unser Dank gilt den Einsendern aus aller Welt, die es uns ermöglicht haben, ein breites, internationales Spektrum der besten Arbeiten zu veröffentlichen. Teilnahmebedingungen für die Graphis-Bücher sind erhältlich bei: **Graphis Inc.**, 307 Fifth Avenue, Tenth Floor, New York, NY 10016. Die aktuellsten Einsendetermine finden Sie unter: www.graphis.com.

Remerciements: Nous remercions les participants du monde entier qui ont rendu possible la publication de cet ouvrage offrant un panorama complet des meilleurs travaux. Les modalités d'inscription peuvent être obtenues auprès de: **Graphis Inc.**, 307 Fifth Avenue, Tenth Floor, New York, NY 10016. Pour les dates limites les plus actuelles consultez www.graphis.com.

opposite: from an ad for Hewlett Packard Color Printers by Goodby, Silverstein & Partners (see page 59)

CommentaryKommentarCommentaire

(opposite) Agency Jung von Matt Werbeagentur GmbH Client Randstad Temp Agency

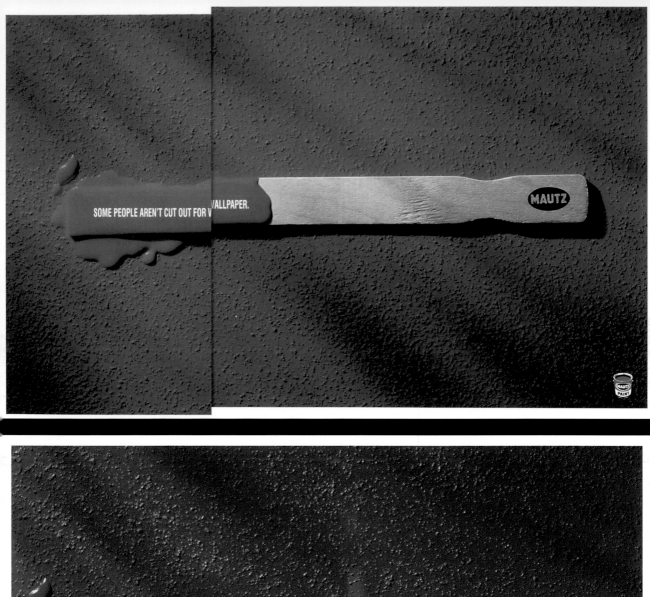

SOME PEOPLE AREN'T CUT OUT FOR WALLPAPER.

MAUTZ

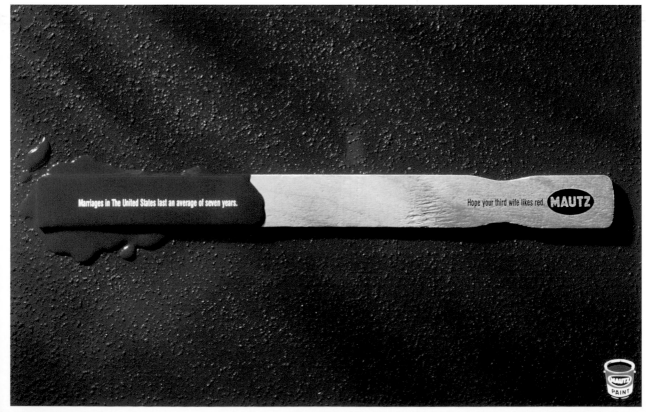

Marriages in The United States last an average of seven years.

Hope your third wife likes red.

MAUTZ

What's Creative? by Tom Jordan

People get excited about great, original ideas. The emphasis isn't just on great... but original. There are three words that can cause instant depression for creatives. They're not "You are fired," "Cancel the shoot" or even "Client killed it." The three words that send defense shields up and can instantly wound the toughest of egos are simply: "It's been done."

There is a clear, distinctive difference between Original Creative, Adaptive Creative and Borrowed Creative. Original Creative finds unique ways to deliver a message. Adaptive Creative adapts a technique or idea from someone or somewhere else outside the world of advertising. Borrowed Creative copies advertising techniques that have been created previously. (There is also Bad Creative that lacks an idea, but I won't get into that.) Original Creative deserves the highest praise. It's work that sets a precedent, is truly unique and stands out. Adaptive Creative uses techniques from television, theater, books, etc. and brings it into advertising. There's nothing wrong with this. But for the creative purist (like a vegetarian who'll eat only fallen fruit) it's considered an easy crutch. Borrowed Creative is cheating. Occasionally it happens by accident, but too often people simply look for techniques and ideas to rip off. As my good friend (and true creative champion) Steve Eichenbaum often says, "Imitation is the sincerest form of plagiarism."

So remember, when looking through wonderful awards books such as this one, please be careful. Don't look to imitate how the ads were executed, but to emulate the brilliance that was applied to solve tough problems.

Was ist kreativ? von Tom Jordan Was Leute gegeistert, sind grossartige, originelle Ideen. Die Betonung liegt dabei vor allem auf originell. Es genügen ein paar wenige Worte, um einen Kreativen auf der Stelle in tiefe Depressionen zu versetzen. Und das sind nicht etwa "Sie sind gefeuert!", "Sagen Sie den Phototermin ab!" oder gar "Der Kunde hat's abgeschmettert!" Die wenigen Worte, die einen Kreativen sofort in die Defensive drängen und auch bei den grössten Egos tiefe Wunden schlagen können, sind ganz einfach: "Das hat's schon gegeben."

Man muss ganz klar zwischen drei Typen von Kreativen unterscheiden - zwischen dem, der erfindet, dem, der adaptiert und dem, der borgt. Der Erste findet eine einzigartige Lösung für die Kommunikation einer Botschaft. Der Zweite übernimmt eine Technik oder Idee von einem Autor oder aus einem Bereich ausserhalb der Werbung. Der Dritte kopiert bereits vorhandene Techniken der Werbung. (Hinzu kommt natürlich noch der schlechte Kreative, der keine Ideen hat, aber darüber will ich mich hier nicht auslassen.)

Der Erfinder verdient das höchste Lob. Seine Arbeit setzt Massstäbe, sie ist einmalig und ragt heraus. Der Adaptierer verwendet Techniken des Fernsehens, des Theaters, der Literatur etc. für die Werbung. Daran ist an sich nichts auszusetzen. Aber für den kreativen Puristen (ähnlich einem Vegetarier, der ausschliesslich Fallobst isst) ist es eine Krücke. Borgen hingegen heisst nichts anderes als mogeln. Hin und wieder passiert es durch Zufall, aber oft genug suchen die Leute einfach nach Techniken und Ideen, die sie abkupfern können. Wie mein guter Freund (er ist ein wahrhaft Kreativer) Steve Eichenbaum oft sagt: "Imitation ist die aufrichtigste Form des Plagiats."

Also denken Sie daran, wenn Sie so wunderbare Jahrbücher wie dieses ansehen, seien Sie vorsichtig. Schauen Sie es sich nicht an, um die Art der Anzeigen zu imitieren, sondern um sich an der Brillanz der Lösungen schwieriger Aufgaben zu orientieren.

Qui sont les créatifs? par Tom Jordan Les gens se passionnent pour les idées grandioses et originales. A la fois grandioses et originales, s'entend. Aussi trois mots ont-ils le pouvoir de démoraliser instantanément un créatif. Non pas «vous êtes renvoyé», «annulez la séance» ni même «le client refuse». Les mots capables de pousser un créatif dans ses retranchements et de battre en brèche sa plus belle assurance sont «cela existe déjà.»

Il faut distinguer trois types de créatifs. Celui qui invente, celui qui adapte et celui qui emprunte. Le premier trouve une manière exclusive de communiquer son message. Le deuxième adapte une technique ou une idée empruntées à un auteur ou à un domaine sans rapport avec la publicité. Le troisième copie les techniques publicitaires déjà existantes. (Sans parler du mauvais créatif qui n'a pas d'idée, mais je ne m'étendrai pas sur ce cas). L'inventeur mérite les éloges les plus vifs. Ses travaux fixent des références. Ils sont uniques et surprenants. L'adaptateur, quant à lui, met les techniques, notamment télévisuelles, théâtrales et livresques au service de la pub. Il n'y a rien à redire à cela. Mais pour le puriste (tel le végétarien qui ne consommerait que des fruits tombés de l'arbre), c'est une solution facile. Emprunter revient à tricher. Cela peut arriver par hasard mais bien trop souvent, le chapardage d'idées et de techniques est intentionnel. Comme mon grand ami (et créatif authentique) Steve Eichenbaum aime à le dire : «L'imitation est la forme la plus sincère du plagiat.»

Aussi, souvenez-vous-en, quand vous feuilletez des annuaires aussi admirables que celui-ci. Et soyez vigilants. Ne cherchez pas à reproduire la manière dont les annonces ont été réalisées. Imprégnez-vous plutôt du génie avec lequel des problèmes complexes ont été résolus.

Opposite: *Mautz Paint advertisement by Hoffman York*

Tom Jordan was born in Cleveland, Ohio, and attended Kent State University. He worked for several small to mid-sized ad agencies, including Leo Barnett and Tatham Laird & Kudner. He currently resides in Milwaukee, Wisconsin, where he has held the position of President & Chief Creative Officer at Hoffman York since 1983. This commentary is an excerpt from his upcoming book, What's a Saatchi... and how come we have two of them?

Tom Jordan wurde in Cleveland, Ohio, geboren und besuchte die Kent State University. Er hat für verschiedene kleine und mittlere Werbeagenturen gearbeitet, darunter Leo Burnett und Taham Laird & Kudner. Gegenwärtig lebt er in Milwaukee, Wisconsin, wo er seit 1983 President und Chief Creative Officer bei Hoffman York ist. Dieser Kommentar ist aus Auszug aus seinem noch unveröffentlichtem Buch What's a Saatchi...and how come we have two of them? *(Was ist ein Saatchi..., und wie kommt es, dass wir zwei davon haben?)*

Tom Jordan est né à Cleveland, dans l'Etat de l'Ohio. Il a fréquenté la Kent State University avant de travailler dans diverses agences de publicité de petite et de moyenne taille telles que Leo Burnett et Taham Laird & Kudner. Il vit actuellement à Milwaukee, dans l'Etat du Wisconsin, où il est directeur et chef de la création chez Hoffman York depuis 1983. Ce commentaire est tiré de son ouvrage à paraître What's a Saatchi.... and how come we have two of them? *(Qu'est-ce qu'un Saatchi .... et comment se fait-il que nous en ayons deux ?)*

opposite: from an ad for Diário Noticias by Edson, FCB , photograph by Atelier De Ilusao (see page 208)

Advertising Annual 2002

Agency **Jean et Moutmarin** Creative Director **Gerard Jean** Art Director **Sebastien Vacherot** Illustrator **Michel Plapla** Copywriter **Manoelle Van Der Vaeren** Client **Land Rover**

FREELANDER V6 - 177 ch

(top) Agency **Jean et Moutmarin** Creative Director **Gerard Jean** Art Director **Herve Barussaud** Photographer **Paul Goirand** (bottom) Agency **Jean et Moutmarin** Creative Director **Gerard Jean** Art Director **Thierry Meunier** Photographer **Denys Vinson** Copywriter **Christopher Trouvé-Dugény** Client **Land Rover** Copywriter **Sidonie Jean** Client **Land Rover**

Automotive 12,13

SOME ARE ATTACHED TO THE OLD WAYS LIKE A BALL IS ATTACHED TO A CHAIN.

You could spend a lifetime gazing at the Carrera 4. That would be a pity. So much more awaits inside. The fluid all-wheel drive. A race-bred 300 horsepower engine. Drive it, and every promise made by that famous shape will be fulfilled. Contact us at 1-800-PORSCHE or porsche.com.

**Looks fast standing still.
That's called truth in packaging.**

Instant freedom, courtesy of the Boxster S. The 250 horsepower boxer engine launches you forward with its distinctive growl. Any memory of life on a leash evaporates in the wind rushing overhead. It's time to run free. Contact us at 1-800-PORSCHE or porsche.com.

**What a dog feels
when the leash breaks.**

The day you go from dreaming about the 911 Carrera Cabriolet to actually owning one is like nothing else. The timeless, flowing lines. The 300 horsepower boxer engine. No, sleep will not come. We suggest a top-down drive in the cool midnight air. Contact us at 1-800-PORSCHE or porsche.com.

**Try going to sleep the first night
you have this in your garage.**

AHH YES

THAT NEW WARRANTY

SMELL

It's a 10-year / 120,000-mile powertrain limited warranty, available on all Isuzu SUVs. It's a warranty no car company can match. That's not to say that car companies can't build durable, long-lasting SUVs. It's just to say that none of them will guarantee it as long as we do. Maybe it's because they have more things to think about than building SUVs. Isuzu. We're not a car company. All we do are trucks. Trucks that are tough enough, and reliable enough, to live up to America's Longest Warranty.

ISUZU
Go farther.

IT'S NO
FAIR-WEATHER
FRIEND

Cars don't want to play on rainy days. Cars don't want to go biking with you, skiing with you, camping with you if it means getting dirty. So we don't make cars. We think you'll get along better with a four-wheel drive Isuzu Rodeo and its Intelligent Suspension Control." It's a truck you can depend on in the rain, the snow, the mud, whatever. And since we back all our SUVs with a 10-year/120,000-mile powertrain limited warranty, America's Longest Warranty, you can be friends for a very long time.

ISUZU
Go farther.

Agency **Goodby, Silverstein & Partners** Creative Directors **Jeffrey Goodby** and **Rich Silverstein** Art Director **Tavia Holmes** Photographer **Michael Rausch** Copywriter **Jeff Huggins** Client **Isuzu**

Agency **TBWA** Art Director **Stephen Cafiero** Photographer **Marc Gouby** Copywriter **Vincent Lobelle** Client **Nissan**

A CDEFGHIJK L NOPQRSTU V XYZ.

BMW Otomobilleri

Borusan Otomotiv
BMW Group Distribütörü
Bayi bilgi hattı:
0800 2190102
www.bmw.com

The Ultimate Driving Machine

Jeep

THERE'S ONLY ONE

McLaughlin, Mike Smith, Jack Neary and Steve Denvir Art Director John Terry Photographer Bill Drummond Copywriter Michael Clowater Typographer John Rodrigues Client DaimlerChrysler Canada Inc.

Agency BBDO Canada Creative Directors Michael

 THE PASSIONATE PURSUIT OF PERFECTION.

The new, more powerful GS 430. A little faster off the line.

0-60 in 4.9 seconds. Bummer.

THE BOSTON SPORTSCAR COMPANY Specializing in the service, repair and restoration of Ferrari sportscars. 781 647 7300

Maybe its time you also got a trophy mechanic.

THE BOSTON SPORTSCAR COMPANY Specializing in the service, repair and restoration of Ferrari sportscars. 781 647 7300

Imagine having a mechanic who scored higher on the SAT than you did.

THE BOSTON SPORTSCAR COMPANY Specializing in the service, repair and restoration of Ferrari sportscars. 781 647 7300

(this page) Agency **Fitzgerald + Company** Creative Director **Jim Paddock** and **Hal Barber** Art Director and Designer **Rob Kottkamp** Photographer **Geoff Knight** Copywriter **Jerry Williams** Client **Boston Sportscar** Automotive 22,23

In Rochester, we have an acute shortage of affordable housing for working people. To help alleviate this problem the Pohlad Family Charities have donated $500,000 to First Homes, an organization committed to building affordable housing. In addition, employees of the Pohlad-owned Marquette Banks are volunteering their time to help in this important cause. Still, there is much more to be done and we need your help. Stop by any Marquette Bank in Rochester and make whatever donation you can. Your dollars, together with the contributions of your friends and neighbors, will make Rochester a great place for all its people to live.

Hayes Creative Director Kerry Krepps Art Director Vincent Stall Photographer Tom Strand Copywriter Tom Hayes Client Marquette Financial Company

KÖLNER BANK
QUALITÄT ZAHLT SICH AUS.

Bullen auf Hausbesuch.
Das Online-Brokerage ist da.

Maybe we did wait too long to offer waxing.

Upstairs @ Prodigy Salon · 282-5099

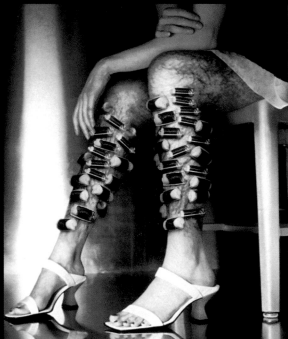

Waxing is now available. Thank you for your patience.

Upstairs @ Prodigy Salon · 282-5099

Sorry for the delay in opening our waxing suite.

Upstairs @ Prodigy Salon · 282-5099

(from top) (1) Agency **The Martin Agency** Creative Directors **Valerie Foley** and **Aurica Green** Art Director **Aurica Green** Photographer **Todd Wright** Copywriter **Valerie Foley** Studio Artist **Matt Wieringo** Account Manager and Print Producer **Aurica Green** (2) Agency **The Martin Agency** Creative Directors **Valerie Foley** and **Aurica Green** Art Director **Aurica Green** Photographer **Todd Wright** Copywriter **Valerie Foley** Studio Artist **Matt Wieringo** (3) Agency **The Martin Agency** Creative Directors **Valerie Foley** and **Aurica Green** Art Director **Aurica Green** Photographer **Todd Wright** Copywriter **Valerie Foley** Print Producer **Aurica Green**

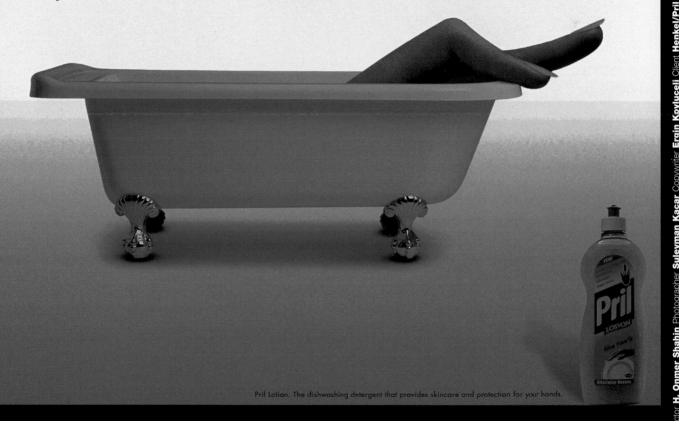

The beauty bath.

Pril Lotion. The dishwashing detergent that provides skincare and protection for your hands.

Derya Tambay Art Director H. Onder Sahin Photographer Süleyman Kaçar Copywriter Ergin Koyluceli Client Henkel/Pril

It could only be Heineken

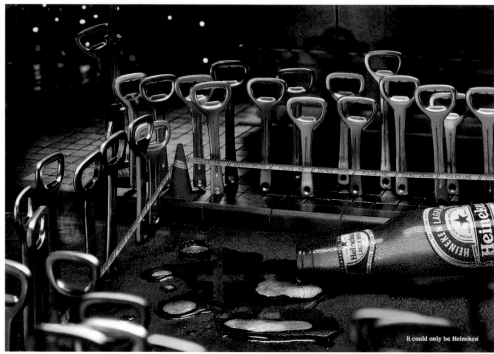

It could only be Heineken

It could only be Heineken

(this spread) Agency **Bates S'pore Pte Ltd.** Creative Director **Aris Theophilakis** Art Directors **Camilla Bjornhaug** and **Preben Moan** Photographer **Erwin Olaf** Client **Heineken Brovwfrijen**

It could only be Heineken

It could only be Heineken

It could only be Heineken

Beverages 30,31

Creative Director **Osualdo Vásquez** Art Director **Jose Muñoz** Designers **Osualdo Vásquez** and **Jose Muñoz** Photographer **Frederick Salgado** Body Painting **Filippo Ioco** Client **Coors Light/V Suarez & Company**

Agency **Wing Latino Group**

Working with nature.

Sometimes unexpected, often

memorable, always satisfying.

'Desert Bird' created in stone by

Peter Grick in the Eastern Sierras,

Lone Pine, California.

'Turning Leaf Zinfandel',

created in California to bring out the

grapes' rich berry character with a delicious

hint of herbs and black pepper.

 Somewhat different wines from the family of Ernest & Julio Gallo

There's pleasure in exploring

where nature ends

and the art begins.

'Tufa stone man' carved by

Theresa Shea at Mono Lake,

Lee Vining, California.

'Turning Leaf Chardonnay',

created in California to give layers of

apple-citrus flavours, tones of vanilla

and an elegant, smooth finish.

Somewhat different wines from the family of Ernest & Julio Gallo

Endless time, patience and

passion, yet probably gone

by the evening end.

'Sand Dolphins' created by

Teresa Shea at Pfeiffer Beach,

Big Sur, California.

'Turning Leaf Chardonnay',

created in California to give layers of

apple-citrus flavours, tones of vanilla

and an elegant, smooth finish.

🍇🍇 Somewhat different wines from the family of Ernest & Julio Gallo®

Half the enjoyment of

working with nature is the

originality of the result.

'Driftwood sculptures' created by

Teresa Shea at Middle Beach,

Point Lobos, California.

'Turning Leaf Cabernet Sauvignon',

created in California to give a delicious

blackberry and cassis character, aged in oak

for increasing depth and complexity.

🍇🍇 Somewhat different wines from the family of Ernest & Julio Gallo®

got chocolate milk?

500 years ago, while others tried to turn lead into gold,
Poland discovered a way to turn rye into vodka.

During the Renaissance, Italian artists
used oil and canvas to create their masterpieces.
The Poles used water and Polish rye.

When crafting our rye vodka,
the only labor saving device we employ is Sunday.

The juggernaut of progress
has been halted at the gates of the distillery.

**WHY A BARTENDER IN SOHO
SHOULD BE CONCERNED WITH THE POTATO HARVEST
IN POLAND.** There is only one luxury potato vodka in the world. Chopin Vodka. Made from the Stobrawa potato,
it has a round, full character with a smooth, clean finish. It is crafted according to a 500-year-old tradition and distilled four times.

CHOPIN   THE WORLD'S ONLY LUXURY POTATO VODKA

POTATOES, WATER, YEAST, In a tiny distillery in Poland, an extraordinary
ALCHEMY. transformation takes place. Stobrawa potatoes become the world's only luxury potato
vodka. Chopin Vodka is crafted slowly, by hand, in accordance with a 500-year-old tradition and distilled four times.

CHOPIN   THE WORLD'S ONLY LUXURY POTATO VODKA

Agency **Clarity Coverdale Fury** Creative Director **Jac Coverdale** Art Director **Glenn Gray** Photographer **William Huber** Copywriter **Kelly Trewartha** Client **Chopin Vodka**   Beverages 36,37

THE 6% CARBOHYDRATE SOLUTION
IN GATORADE® SPEEDS FLUIDS
AND CARBOHYDRATES INTO
THE BLOODSTREAM.

WHAT THAT REALLY MEANS:

IT INJECTS LIFE BACK
INTO YOUR GAME.

THERE'S A REASON THIS STUFF WAS CREATED.

is *it* in you?

PURE MALT
VOUS ÊTES SUR LES TERRES
DU CLAN CAMPBELL

L'ABUS D'ALCOOL EST DANGEREUX POUR LA SANTÉ, CONSOMMEZ AVEC MODÉRATION.

PURE MALT
VOUS ÊTES SUR LES TERRES
DU CLAN CAMPBELL

L'ABUS D'ALCOOL EST DANGEREUX POUR LA SANTÉ, CONSOMMEZ AVEC MODÉRATION.

Agency **Bddp & Fils** Art Director **Damien Bellon** Photographer **Marc Gouby** Copywriter **Bruno Delhomme** Client **Clan-Campbell**

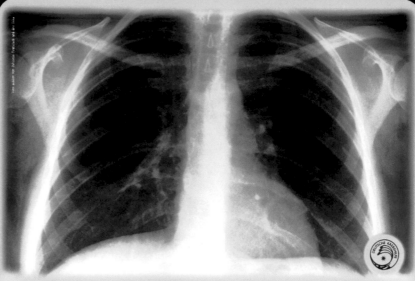

Wissen Sie wirklich,
wie es in Ihrem Innersten
aussieht?

Früherkennung rettet Leben.
www.krebshilfe.de

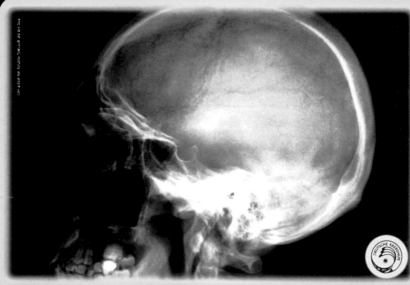

Wissen Sie wirklich,
wie es in Ihrem Innersten
aussieht?

Früherkennung rettet Leben.
www.krebshilfe.de

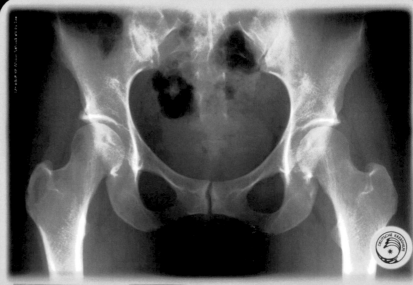

Wissen Sie wirklich,
wie es in Ihrem Innersten
aussieht?

Früherkennung rettet Leben.
www.krebshilfe.de

ACCIDENTS HAPPEN WHERE YOU LEAST EXPECT IT. DRIVE CAREFULLY.

DN SAFE ROAD

pictures that stick

pictures that stick

pictures that stick

Polaroid
i-zone

pictures that stick

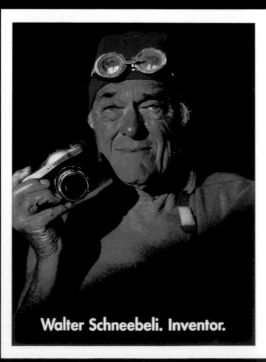

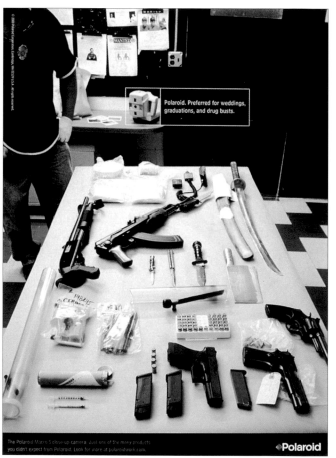

Agency **Clarity Coverdale Fury** Creative Director **Jac Coverdale** Art Director and Copywriter **Mark Sorensen** Client **770 Radio K**

WHICH SPORTSCENTER DO YOU WATCH?
5 AM – 12 PM, 6 PM, 11 PM, 1 AM, 2 AM ET

NOMAR GARCIAPARRA WATCHES THE 6 PM SPORTSCENTER.

WHICH SPORTSCENTER DO YOU WATCH?
5 AM – 12 PM, 6 PM, 11 PM, 1 AM, 2 AM ET

THE GRETZKY FAMILY WATCHES THE 11 AM SPORTSCENTER.

WHICH SPORTSCENTER DO YOU WATCH?
5 AM – 12 PM, 6 PM, 11 PM, 1 AM, 2 AM ET

VINCE CARTER WATCHES THE 1 AM SPORTSCENTER.

Agency **W+K** Creative Directors **Michael Prieve** and **Stacy Wall** Art Director **Matt Stein** Photographer **Matt Jones** Copywriter **Jon Goldberg** Client **ESPN** Communications 50,51

A few helpful numbers from Nokia.
Proud sponsor of the Verizon Byron Nelson Classic.

NOKIA
CONNECTING PEOPLE
www.Nokia.com

It's me. What's shakin'?... Oh, really? Did you turn in your lineup already?... Man, I won my league two years ago, but injuries are just killing me this season... Yeah, like I can predict a torn ACL and two concussions when I'm drafting... Me too. I drew the thirteenth spot this year, so all the stars were gone. I got some decent guys, but, man, I'm tellin' you, injuries have just leveled me. I'm having to start all my bottom-feeders. Anyway, that's not what I was calling about... Well, about tomorrow... It doesn't look good... No, I'm not chickening out, I just... Oh, please. I'm not the guy who squealed when he got a little blood on his shirt... Dude, it was a scratch... No, Dickinson was the one who was really hurtin'. Did you know he had knee surgery like a month later?... Yeah, you might be able to cover him now... Right. You can't even... No, I want to play, but... No, she didn't. Well, yeah, she did, but only because she had other plans for us tomorrow. It's not like... Okay... Okay, you done?... Very funny. That's funny stuff, man. You should take that on the road... What do you mean? She's not the boss. I'm not the boss either. It's all about compromise, man... I tried. She didn't bite... I tried that too... Yeah, yeah, yeah. I tried everything. It's not gonna happen, man... No, you can't call the whole thing off. Why would you do that?... Why?... Call Stewart... Patterson then... I don't know. Surely you know somebody who can play... No, don't call him. He bugs me... I don't care. I'll be there next week, and I don't want to have to put up with him... Yes, he will. You can't just invite somebody for one game and then, "Thanks for coming, we'll call you if we're desperate again." That's not cool... It doesn't matter. It's still not cool... I didn't put you in this situation. Apparently, I'm not the only one who... I already tried that, man. She won't budge... Why would I do that? Have you ever even dealt with a woman before?... Well, it's no wonder. Man, you've got a lot to learn... There you go again. Okay, let me ask you this: if it makes me less of a man to sit out one game, what does it make you for missing a whole month last year... Flu, schmoo... Okay, whatever. You can yap all you want. It still doesn't change anything... Listen to me. Tomorrow is not gonna happen for me. I'll be back next week... Yes, I swear... I'll be there... Yes, I've already cleared it with her, thank you... Ha ha... Okay, let me know who wins... Yes, I'll be there next week... Okay. See you tomorrow. I mean next week... Yeah, yeah. Whatever... Okay. Take it easy... Later.

Make a long story short.

With a new Nokia 5100 Series wireless phone, you can send mobile messages from phone to phone. You can also send e-mail and choose from a variety of Xpress-on™ color covers. So express yourself, in as few words as possible.

NOKIA
CONNECTING PEOPLE
www.Nokia.com

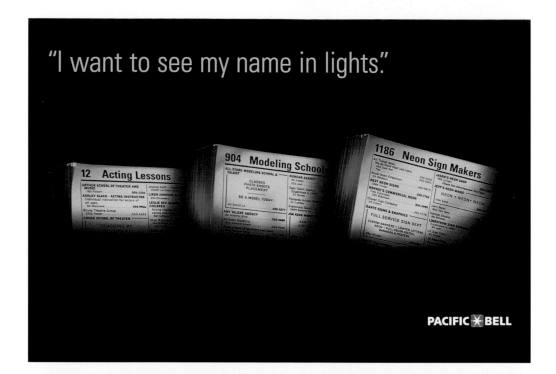

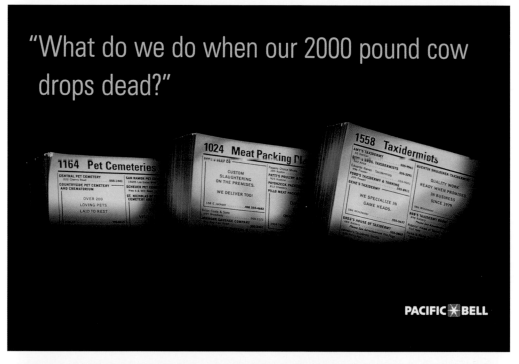

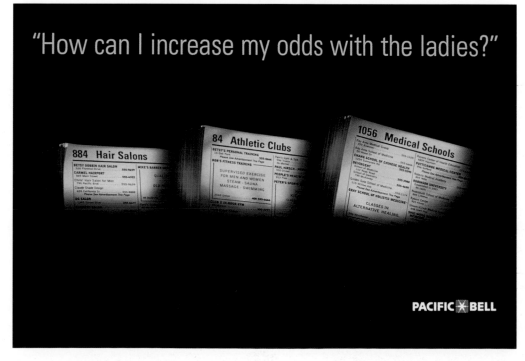

(this page) Agency **Goodby, Silverstein & Partners** Creative Director **Greg Bell** Art Director **Peter Nicholson** Photographer **Darrell Williams** Copywriter **Chris Ford** Client **Pacific Bell Yellow Pages** Communications 54, 55

MOVISTAR ACTIVA IN USA.
USE YOUR MOBILE IN MORE THAN 100 COUNTRIES.

Telefónica
MoviStar

MOVISTAR ACTIVA IN SWITZERLAND.
USE YOUR MOBILE IN MORE THAN 100 COUNTRIES.

Telefónica
MoviStar

That great plan for a business you've been saving?
It's time to let it out into the world. Because now everyone can
play in the emerging e-services economy. Your rainy day idea
can team up with someone else's rainy day idea, or everyone else's
rainy day idea. And hp servers, storage, software and consulting
will help tie them all together. Do you have a business in you?
Invent it here: www.hp.com/e-services

The Grand Opening of You.
e-services solutions from hp.

Go David.

Look big. Compete globally. Run circles around your competitors with your vast enthusiasm and technical
savvy. Show the world what you have to offer. Join the e-services economy. www.hp.com/david
Start-ups playing big. e-services solutions from hp.

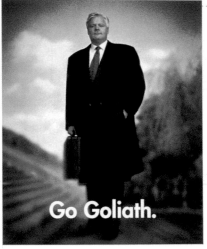

Go Goliath.

Be nimble. Be quick. Run circles around your competitors with your vast experience and technical
savvy. Show the world what you have to offer. Join the e-services economy. www.hp.com/goliath.
Big business getting nimble. e-services solutions from hp.

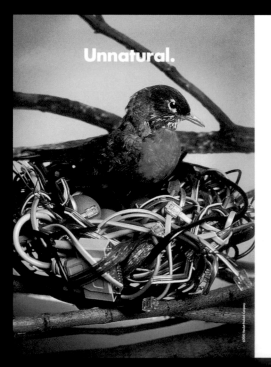

Unnatural.

Tangles of wires and cords aren't part of anyone's master plan.
A return to simplicity is on the way, in the form of a new e-services solution:
hp printers and portable devices with Bluetooth wireless technology.
Bluetooth allows walk-up beaming of documents to a printer from your PDA, laptop,
cell phone, or digital camera (or from one portable device to another).
It's hp printing without wires—even among different platforms and programs.
By adapting to the world's different digital environments,
Bluetooth ensures success whenever you fly off somewhere.
See how we're reinventing the workplace for the e-services economy.
At www.e-services.hp.com

Take to the air.
e-services solutions from hp.

True to the original.
Surprise. Realism you can almost slice.
Vibrant color. Printouts true to your original photos.
Introducing the new hp DeskJet 970C.

True to the original.
The play of light and shadow
The rich colors of life
Printouts like your original photos
The new hp DeskJet 970C

True to the original.
Don't blink. It serves a quick ten pages
per minute of stunning realism. With printouts
that are most like your original photos.
The new hp DeskJet 970C

STRENGTH MEETS SPIRIT | We're Progress Energy. A new company comprised of CP&L Energy and Florida Progress. We supply electricity, broadband capacity and natural gas to one of the nation's highest population growth areas. So, although we're structured for stability, we have no intention of standing still.

Progress Energy

STABILITY MEETS SPUNK | We're Progress Energy. A new company comprised of CP&L Energy and Florida Progress. We supply electricity, broadband capacity and natural gas to one of the nation's highest population growth areas. So, although we're structured for stability, we have no intention of standing still.

Progress Energy

STURDINESS MEETS HUSTLE | We're Progress Energy. A new company comprised of CP&L Energy and Florida Progress. We supply electricity, broadband capacity and natural gas to one of the nation's highest population growth areas. So, although we're structured for stability, we have no intention of standing still.

◈ **Progress Energy**

CANCEL A FLIGHT WITH OVER 500 PASSENGERS, AND
YOU'LL BE IN A WHOLE NEW FIELD OF TRANSPORTATION.

One sure way to watch the wheels of commerce turn is to delay or divert a super-wide-body plane. Suddenly hundreds of people will need ground-based transportation, all on your airline's nickel. To prevent that from happening to your A380 and Boeing 747X-Stretch flights, we're creating the most reliable family of engines possible, built on the heritage of two great companies. As a result, your airplanes will taxi, instead of your passengers. Call 513-552-3316 or visit www.enginealliance.com to learn more about the dependable GP7000.

Alliance
A joint company of GE Aircraft Engines and Pratt & Whitney

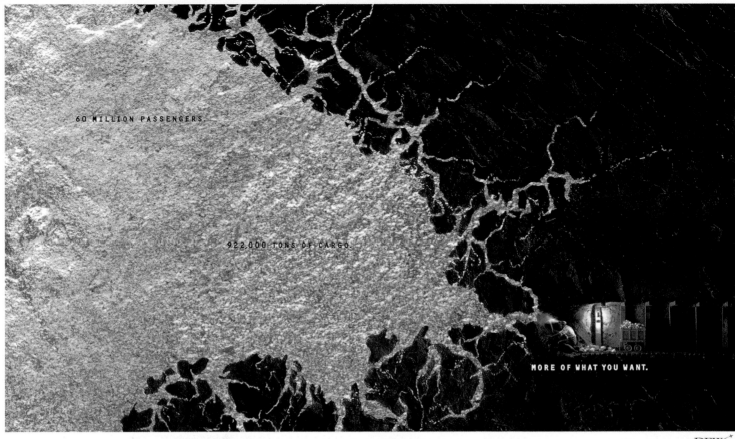

60 MILLION PASSENGERS.

922,000 TONS OF CARGO.

MORE OF WHAT YOU WANT.

{ Tons and tons of opportunity. That's what's waiting for you in the heart of the booming economic center known as the Dallas/Fort Worth   Metroplex. To tap into it, call Jeff Fegan, executive director, at (800) 521-4296 or log on to dfwairport.com. }

DFW
INTERNATIONAL
AIRPORT

Accepted at *The Second City*.

The Discover®Card is accepted at 1000 new locations every day including *Eddie Bauer*

The Discover®Card is accepted at 1000 new locations every day including **THE SHARPER IMAGE**

The Discover®Card is accepted at 1000 new locations every day including **TOURNEAU**

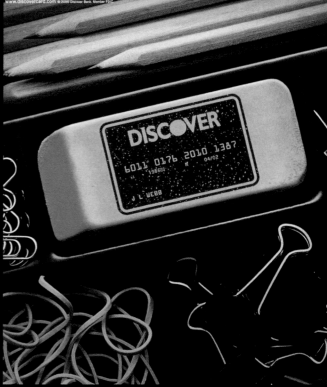

The Discover®Card is accepted at 1000 new locations every day including

DISCOVER
C L A S S I C

A CARD NUMBER AS IMPOSSIBLE
TO READ AS THAT THING YOU
CALL A SIGNATURE.

J L WEBB

FACT: YOU CAN'T STEAL SOMETHING THAT'S NOT THERE. That's the idea behind Discover Card's newest technology,
DeskShop: Each time you shop on-line, you can automatically generate a substitute number, preventing your actual
Discover Card account number from ever appearing on the Web. Just click a button and a virtual number pops into place.
It even fills out the rest of the form for you. Smart, huh? DISCOVER CARD. FOR THE SLIGHTLY SMARTER CONSUMER.

Only at www.Discovercard.com

DISCOVER
C L A S S I C

SEE THIS NUMBER?
YEAH, WELL NEITHER
CAN E-THIEVES.

J L WEBB

FACT: YOU CAN'T STEAL SOMETHING THAT'S NOT THERE. That's the idea behind Discover Card's newest technology,
DeskShop: Each time you shop on-line, you can automatically generate a substitute number, preventing your actual
Discover Card account number from ever appearing on the Web. Just click a button and a virtual number pops into place.
It even fills out the rest of the form for you. Smart, huh? DISCOVER CARD. FOR THE SLIGHTLY SMARTER CONSUMER.

Only at www.Discovercard.com

(this page) Agency **ChM/BBDO** Art Director **Cedric Hardoutiounian** Photographer **Marc Gouby** Copywriter **Benoit Sahores** Client **FedEx**

Camponesa Steak-House. Now delivering. Orders Between 12am to 22pm. Call (01) 469 0328

Brown. Official courier colour of Gold, Silver and Bronze.

Worldwide Olympic Partner

What you do in the morning is your business.
Getting your products to customers first is ours.

It's relaxing to know our guaranteed 8 a.m. delivery will get your products into the marketplace ahead of the competition. And you can bask in the knowledge that our Early A.M. service delivers to twice as many ZIP Codes as anyone else. So start the day by letting us help you stretch your market share. All other stretching is strictly up to you. Call 1-800-PICK-UPS or visit ups.com

MOVING at the SPEED of BUSINESS.

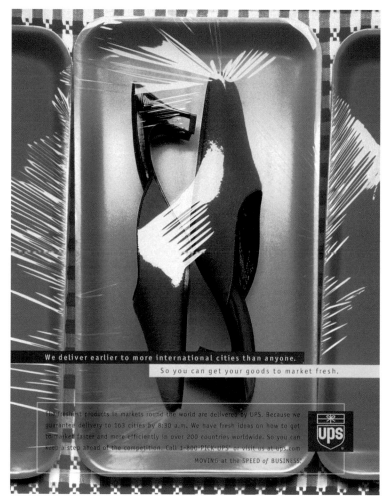

We deliver earlier to more international cities than anyone.
So you can get your goods to market fresh.

The freshest products in markets round the world are delivered by UPS. Because we guarantee delivery to 163 cities by 8:30 a.m. We have fresh ideas on how to get to market faster and more efficiently in over 200 countries worldwide. So you can keep a step ahead of the competition. Call 1-800-PICK-UPS or visit us at ups.com

MOVING at the SPEED of BUSINESS.

(this page) Agency **Lowe Lintas & Partners** Creative Directors **Lee Garfinkel** and **Gary Goldsmith** Art Director **Hank Kosinski** Designers **Rob Feakins** and **Roger Bentley** Copywriter **John Maxham** Creative Coordinator **Gabby Rosedale** Client **UPS Delivery Services** 70, 71

NEW CLASSES BEGIN SEPTEMBER 4TH. REGISTER BY PHONE NOW.

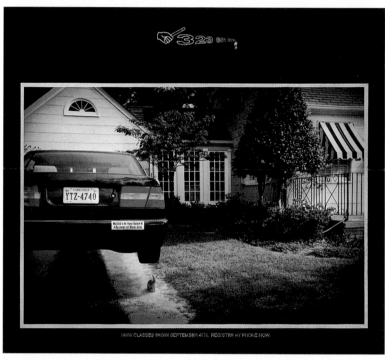

NEW CLASSES BEGIN SEPTEMBER 4TH. REGISTER BY PHONE NOW.

NEW CLASSES BEGIN SEPTEMBER 4TH. REGISTER BY PHONE NOW.

(this page) Agency **Siddall, Matus & Coughter** Creative Director **Shari Hindman** Art Director **Chris Nott** Photographers **Kip Dawkins** and **John Henley** Copywriter **David Neale** Client **Academy of Magic Arts**   Education 72,73

Pioneer

EVERYTHING ELSE COMES SECOND.

For some, a home theater system comes before everything. Even food and water. They're the ones we created our DV-434 DVD player for. Its Digital Progressive Scan output creates a picture that'll make you wonder why anybody still watches videotape. And like all our equipment it's built to withstand almost anything, including frostbite.

pioneerelectronics.com

PUSH A BUTTON. ~~PUSH IT AGAIN.~~ ~~REALIZE THAT YOUR COMPUTER~~ ~~HAS BEEN DISCONNECTED FROM~~ ~~THE INTERNET. RELOAD YOUR~~ ~~SERVER. GET A BUSY SIGNAL.~~ ~~GET ANGRY. GET BACK ON THE~~ ~~INTERNET. ENTER PASSWORD~~ ~~AGAIN. WAIT.~~ READ E-MAIL.

Your life just got simpler. Introducing the i-opener. Instant access to the Internet and e-mail at the push of a button — all without a computer. And at $99, it's never been easier to make the Internet part of your daily life.

www.netpliance.com

TAKE OUT OF THE BOX. ~~READ~~ ~~THE COMPLICATED INSTRUCTION~~ ~~MANUAL. BECOME EXTREMELY~~ ~~CONFUSED. CALL TECH SUPPORT.~~ ~~WAIT FIFTEEN MINUTES ON HOLD.~~ ~~GIVE UP. PAY SOME NERD TO~~ ~~COME SET UP YOUR COMPUTER~~ ~~FOR YOU.~~ ENJOY THE INTERNET.

Your life just got simpler. Introducing the i-opener. Instant access to the Internet and e-mail at the push of a button — all without a computer. And at $99, it's never been easier to make the Internet part of your daily life.

www.netpliance.com

Sounds so good you won't want to leave your car.

Why put up with your old tape deck when you can have digital sound in your car, from a leader in car audio technology.
Pioneer car CD stereos use Mosfet amplification to deliver crystal clear sound without any distortion, just like you'd expect from your own hi-fi system. So, when you install a Pioneer car CD system you'll feel right at home, literally.

Pioneer

Sounds so good you won't want to leave your car.

Why put up with your old tape deck when you can have digital sound in your car, from a leader in car audio technology.
Pioneer car CD stereos use Mosfet amplification to deliver crystal clear sound without any distortion, just like you'd expect from your own hi-fi system. So, when you install a Pioneer car CD system you'll feel right at home, literally.

Pioneer

Sounds so good you won't want to leave your car.

Why put up with your old tape deck when you can have digital sound in your car, from a leader in car audio technology.
Pioneer car CD stereos use Mosfet amplification to deliver crystal clear sound without any distortion, just like you'd expect from your own hi-fi system. So, when you install a Pioneer car CD system you'll feel right at home, literally.

Pioneer

(this page) Agency **Batey Ads** Creative Directors **Rodd Chant** and **Richard Copping** Art Director **Richard Copping** Photographer **Stephen Stewart** Copywriter **Rodd Chant** Retouching **Electric Art** Client **Pioneer**

Electronics 76,77

See what happens when writers
take on the toughest client of all:

Themselves.

The "What I'd Be Doing If It Paid As Well As Advertising" Show

Art Director **Doug Pedersen** Copywriter **Curtis Smith** Client The One Club for Art & Copy

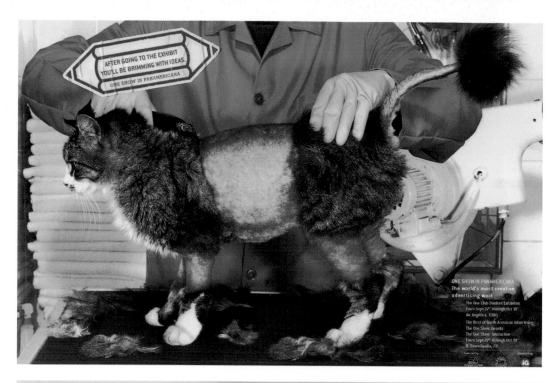

(this page) Agency **DM9 DDB** Creative Directors **Erh Ray, Camila Franco** and **Sergio Valente** Art Directors **Paulo Diehl** and **Teca Guarita** Photographer **Guto Seixas** Copywriters **Alessandra Pereira** and **Flavio Casarotti** Client **One Show Exhibition**

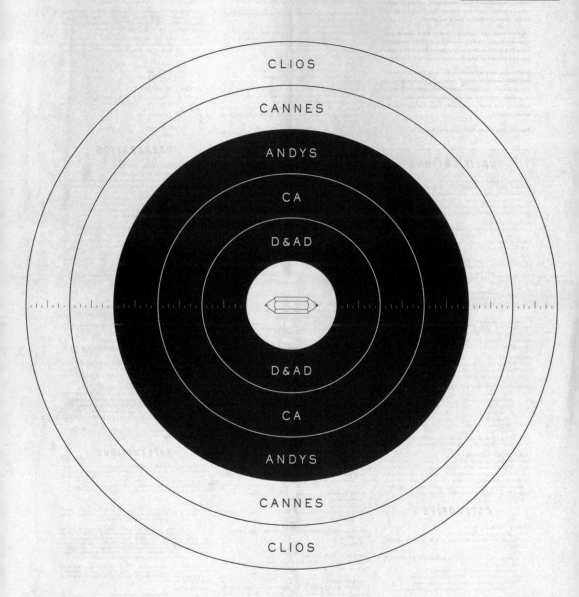

THE SHOW 2000 CALL FOR ENTRIES

Agency **Clarity Coverdale Fury** Creative Director **Jac Coverdale** Art Director **Glenn Gray** Photographer **Chris Sheehan** Copywriter **Troy Longie** Client **Advertising Federation of Minnesota** Events 80, 81

AND YOU THOUGHT HARVARD OR M.I.T. WERE HARD SCHOOLS TO GET INTO.

Announcing the Technical Diving Conference at the Special Forces Underwater Operations School. For the very first time in history, the civilian and military communities will converge in Key West to delve into the realm of technical diving. Truly an unprecedented event, the conference will cover such topics as decompression modeling, exploration dives (with a display of the Andrea Doria by its owner, John Moyer), and all other aspects of technical diving. So join us for this amazing exchange of information within the extreme diving community October 4th-8th. Call 1 800 553-NAUI or visit www.naui.org to sign up.

EVOLUTION OF MAN. COMPLETE.

| 1960 | NAUI celebrates 40 years of expert underwater instruction and education | 2000 |

Where: Houston, TX Memorial Center
When: Nov. 10th-12th 1 800-553-NAUI

Join us this November as we proudly celebrate the sport of scuba diving with our 40th anniversary. A well-deserved tribute to all who know that the human body cannot exist without water.

PG. 43

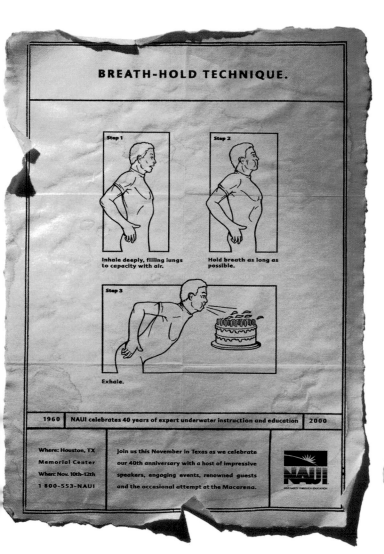

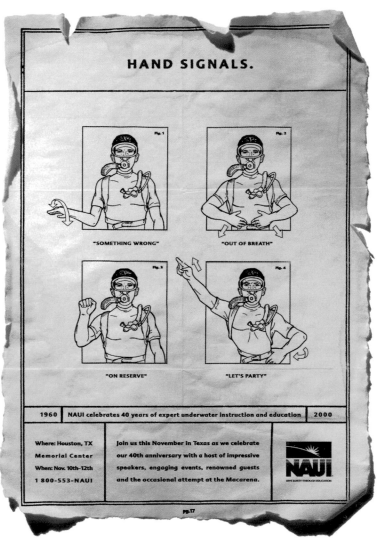

GOOD JUDGEMENT / INHIBITIONS / BLOOD ALCOHOL CONTENT / MOTOR SKILLS

the absolute music bash

Join us Thursday, Feb.1 at Linguini and Bob from 5 p.m. until midnight. It'll be a night to remember. For some, anyway.

Ameren UE

PROUD SPONSOR OF THE SAINT LOUIS ART FAIR.

www.ameren.com

(this spread) Agency **Energy Project Group** Creative and Art Director **Nikko Amandonico** Photographer **Terry Richardson** Client **Sisley (Benetton Group)**

SISLEY

SEPARATED AT BIRTH

nike.com/AirBeschutzVIII

GETS YOU MOVING QUICKLY

nike.com/AirFlightMotion

OH SO SNUG

nike.com/AirKukini

Fashion 90,91 (this page) Agency Goodby, Silverstein & Partners Creative Directors Jeffrey Goodby and Rich Silverstein Art Directors Paul Hirsch, Claude Shade and Josh Denberg Copywriters Josh Denberg Photographer Kenji Toma Client Nike

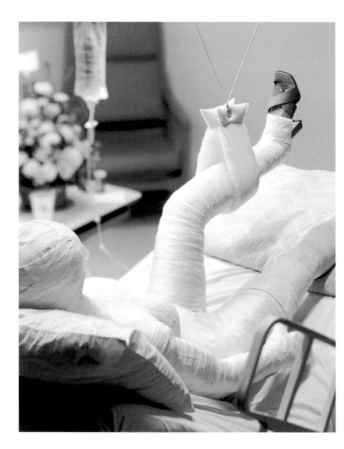

Obsessively shoe obsessed  Madeline

Obsessively shoe obsessed  Madeline

Obsessively shoe obsessed  Madeline

(this spread) Agency **Goodby, Silverstein & Partners** Creative Directors **Jeffrey Goodby** and **Rich Silverstein** Art Director **Margaret Johnson** Photographer **Thierry LeGoues** Copywriter **Steve Payonzeck** Client **Nike**

Agency **Jean & Montmarin** Creative Director **Gérard Jean** Art Directors **Rémi Courgeon** and **Hervé Barrussaud** Copywriter **Sidonie Jean** Photographer **Benny Valsson** Client **Lee Cooper**

CLIENT	CODE
Mail	33150
mmercial	33240
omotions	36059
dustrial	37540
rp. Issues	39054
ade	40190
ernet Svc.	40335
operties	44640
obal Grp.	48910
orldwide	50225
ernational	55430
ofessional	56740
Response	59090
s. Afffairs	60155
onsorship	60196
b. Serv	70120
lidays	75035
k	75076
rsonal	88221
sc.	88870
APPROVAL	

EMPLOYEE # 2840   **EMPLOYEE NAME**   **WEEK ENDING**

DAY	7:00	8:00	9:00	10:00	11:00	12:00	1:00	2:00	3:00	4:00	5:00	6:00	7:00	8:00	9:00	10:00	11:00	12:00	TOTAL
WEEK 1																			
MON																			
TUES																			
WED																			
THUR																			
FRI																			
SAT																			
SUN																			
TOTAL																			
WEEK 2																			
MON																			
TUES																			
WED																			
THUR																			
FRI																			
SAT																			
SUN																			
TOTAL																			

(TIME — OVERTIME)

Just do it

john varvatos

john varvatos

„MEINE STRELITZIA ZEIGT STIL. WAS ZEIGE ICH?"

IS THIS:

A) LITTLE RED RIDING HOOD VISITING
   HER GRANDMA IN QUEENS

B) THE LATEST FROM DONNA KARAN

C) A MAN WITH A LATE-NIGHT
   HANKERING FOR SQUASH

eLUXURY.com *Know what is, know what isn't.*
Find the finest brands and the latest fashion news from the insiders at www.eLUXURY.com.
An affiliate of LVMH Moët Hennessy Louis Vuitton—the world's leading luxury-products group.

IS THIS:

A) LINGERIE FRIDAY AT A BIG FIVE
   ACCOUNTING FIRM

B) BILLY THE INTERN'S LUCKY DAY

C) THE LATEST FROM LA PERLA

eLUXURY.com *Know what is, know what isn't.*
Find the finest brands and the latest fashion news from the insiders at www.eLUXURY.com.
An affiliate of LVMH Moët Hennessy Louis Vuitton—the world's leading luxury-products group.

IS THIS:

A) BEHAVIOR THAT GETS YOU KICKED OUT
   OF THE LION TAMERS UNION

B) THE REASON KIDS RUN AWAY
   AND JOIN THE CIRCUS

C) THE LATEST FROM MICHAEL KORS

eLUXURY.com *Know what is, know what isn't.*
Find the finest brands and the latest fashion news from the insiders at www.eLUXURY.com.
An affiliate of LVMH Moët Hennessy Louis Vuitton—the world's leading luxury-products group.

Forget the lines.
Anything is possible.

PFPC
A member of The PNC Financial Services Group

Solutions to stay out front.

Our Global Fund Services: Accounting • Administration • Transfer Agency • Shareholder Services
Advanced Output Solutions • Custody • Securities Lending • Integrated Banking Transaction Services
Retirement Services • Alternative Investment Services • Offshore Fund Services • Subaccounting Services

Phone 302-791-2000 • www.pfpc.com

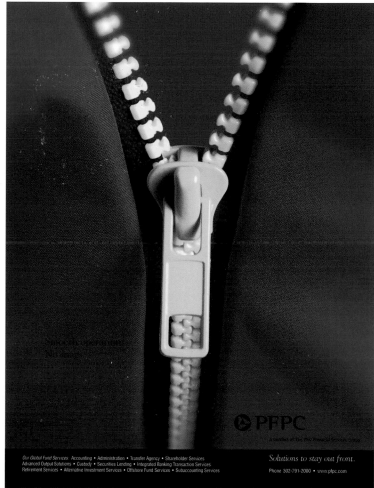

PFPC
A member of The PNC Financial Services Group

Solutions to stay out front.

Our Global Fund Services: Accounting • Administration • Transfer Agency • Shareholder Services
Advanced Output Solutions • Custody • Securities Lending • Integrated Banking Transaction Services
Retirement Services • Alternative Investment Services • Offshore Fund Services • Subaccounting Services

Phone 302-791-2000 • www.pfpc.com

(this page) Agency **Mangos** Creative Director **Bradley Gast** Art Director **Jeff Scott** Photographer **Skip Caplan** Copywriter **Jan Lawrence** Client: **PFPC**

Client **Campbell Soup Company Ltd.**

BBDO Canada Creative Directors **Jack McLaughlin, David Houghton, Jack Neary** and **Craig Redmond** Art Directors **David Houghton** and **Richard Mirabelli** Photographer **Per Kristiansen** Copywriters **Craig Redmond, David Bonner** and **Eric Parker**

Haste doesn't always make waste. Occasionally it makes this delightful stir fry.
ORANGE CHICKEN AND VEGETABLE STIR FRY
Ingredients:
1 tbsp vegetable oil 15mL
1 lb boneless, skinless chicken breasts, cut in 3" (7 cm) strips 500g
2 cups fresh or frozen broccoli florets 500mL
2 cloves garlic, minced or 1/4 tsp (1mL) garlic powder
1 can (10 oz/284 mL) CAMPBELL'S® Condensed Cream of Chicken or Half Fat Cream of Chicken Soup
1 can (10 oz/284 mL) mandarin orange segments
1/4 tsp dried oregano flakes 1mL
4 cups hot cooked rice 1L
Prep/Cook Time: 25 minutes
Heat oil at medium-high in large skillet or wok. Add chicken and stir fry 5 minutes or until browned; set aside. Reduce heat to medium.
Add broccoli and garlic to skillet; stir fry 2 minutes (or add garlic powder to mixture in next step).
Stir in soup, liquid drained from mandarin orange segments (reserve segments) and oregano. Heat to a boil, stirring often. Reduce heat to low.
Add in chicken. Simmer until chicken is cooked through - about 5 minutes. Stir in orange segments. Serve with rice. Serves 4.
Tip: For added convenience, substitute 2 cups frozen vegetable mixture for broccoli.
For more great recipe ideas, visit us at www.campbellsoup.ca
©2000 C.S.C. Ltd. trademark licensee.
GOOD FOOD FAST. Campbell's

Running around like a chicken with its head cut off? Let's talk soup.
CHICKEN AND STUFFING SKILLET
Ingredients:
1 tbsp vegetable oil 15mL
1 lb boneless, skinless chicken breasts, cut in cubes 500g
1 box (120 g) stuffing mix
1 cup each, finely diced carrots and celery 250mL
1 can (10oz/284 mL) CAMPBELL'S® Condensed Cream of Mushroom or Half Fat Cream of Mushroom Soup
1/2 cup milk 125mL
1/2 cup shredded Cheddar cheese 125mL
Prep/Cook Time: 30 minutes
Heat oil at medium-high in large skillet. Add chicken, cook 10 minutes or until browned and cooked through; set aside. Reduce heat to medium.
Prepare stuffing according to package directions in skillet, adding carrots and celery to water with seasoning.
Top with chicken. Mix soup and milk. Pour over chicken. Sprinkle with cheese and stir gently. Cover and heat through at low heat. Serves 4.
Tip: For added convenience, substitute 3 cups cooked, cubed chicken or turkey for uncooked chicken. Reduce cook time in first step to 2 min.
For more great recipe ideas, visit us at www.campbellsoup.ca
©2000 C.S.C. Ltd. trademark licensee.
GOOD FOOD FAST. Campbell's

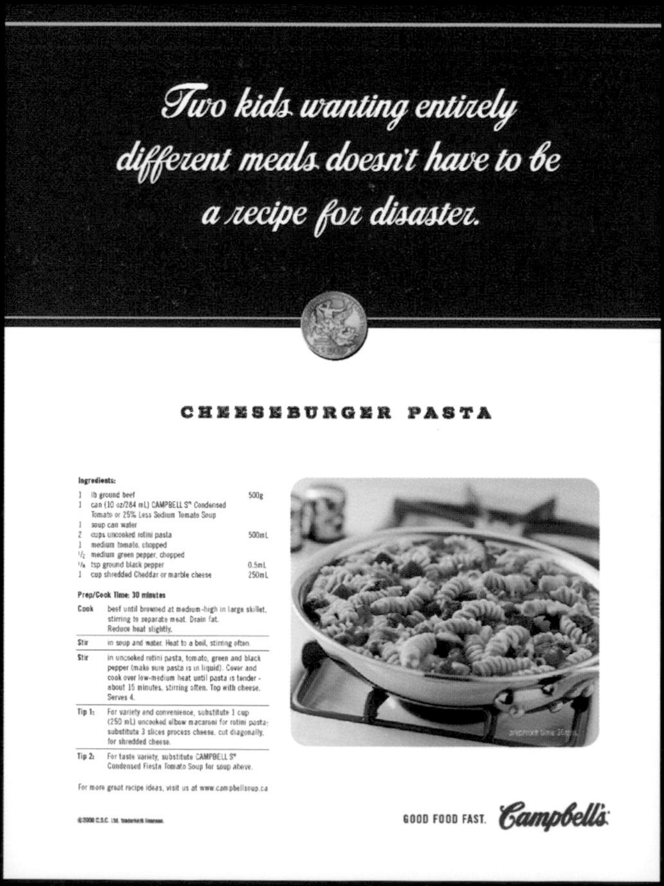
Two kids wanting entirely different meals doesn't have to be a recipe for disaster.
CHEESEBURGER PASTA
Ingredients:
1 lb ground beef 500g
1 can (10 oz/284 mL) CAMPBELL'S® Condensed Tomato or 25% Less Sodium Tomato Soup
1 soup can water
2 cups uncooked rotini pasta 500mL
1 medium tomato, chopped
1/2 medium green pepper, chopped
1/8 tsp ground black pepper 0.5mL
1 cup shredded Cheddar or marble cheese 250mL
Prep/Cook Time: 30 minutes
Cook beef until browned at medium-high in large skillet, stirring to separate meat. Drain fat. Reduce heat slightly.
Stir in soup and water. Heat to a boil, stirring often.
Stir in uncooked rotini pasta, tomato, green and black pepper (make sure pasta is in liquid). Cover and cook over low-medium heat until pasta is tender - about 15 minutes, stirring often. Top with cheese. Serves 4.
Tip 1: For variety and convenience, substitute 1 cup (250 mL) uncooked elbow macaroni for rotini pasta; substitute 3 slices process cheese, cut diagonally, for shredded cheese.
Tip 2: For taste variety, substitute CAMPBELL'S® Condensed Fiesta Tomato Soup for soup above.
For more great recipe ideas, visit us at www.campbellsoup.ca
©2000 C.S.C. Ltd. trademark licensee.
GOOD FOOD FAST. Campbell's

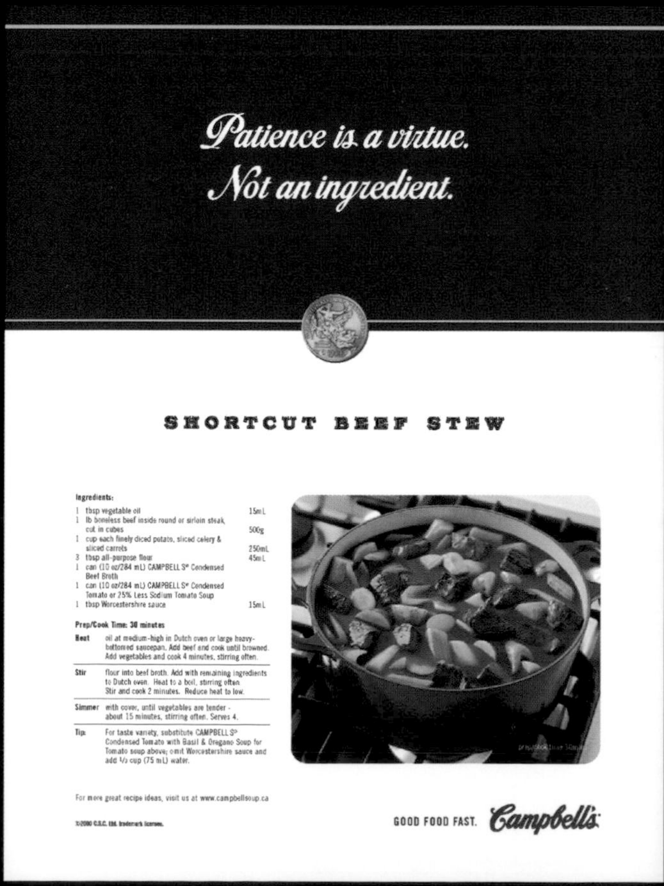
Patience is a virtue. Not an ingredient.
SHORTCUT BEEF STEW
Ingredients:
1 tbsp vegetable oil 15mL
1 lb boneless beef inside round or sirloin steak, cut in cubes 500g
1 cup each finely diced potato, sliced celery & sliced carrots 250mL
3 tbsp all-purpose flour 45mL
1 can (10 oz/284 mL) CAMPBELL'S® Condensed Beef Broth
1 can (10 oz/284 mL) CAMPBELL'S® Condensed Tomato or 25% Less Sodium Tomato Soup
1 tbsp Worcestershire sauce 15mL
Prep/Cook Time: 30 minutes
Heat oil at medium-high in Dutch oven or large heavy-bottomed saucepan. Add beef and cook until browned. Add vegetables and cook 4 minutes, stirring often.
Stir flour into beef broth. Add with remaining ingredients to Dutch oven. Heat to a boil, stirring often. Stir and cook 2 minutes. Reduce heat to low.
Simmer with cover, until vegetables are tender - about 15 minutes, stirring often. Serves 4.
Tip: For taste variety, substitute CAMPBELL'S® Condensed Tomato with Basil & Oregano Soup for Tomato soup above; omit Worcestershire sauce and add 1/3 cup (75 mL) water.
For more great recipe ideas, visit us at www.campbellsoup.ca
©2000 C.S.C. Ltd. trademark licensee.
GOOD FOOD FAST. Campbell's

Parmalat Ice Cream.
100% pure milk.

Visit our shop at Rua do Beco Torto, nº1, Cascais.   **gelataria**   parmalat

THINK GLOBALLY. SPOON LOCALLY.

GET YOUR SOY WITH SILK.

A TASTE BUD LOVEFEST.

GET YOUR SOY WITH SILK.

HAVE A NICE LIFE SPAN.

GET YOUR SOY WITH SILK.

TASTE AND NUTRITION CO-HABITATE HARMONIOUSLY.

GET YOUR SOY WITH SILK.

(this page) Agency **Carmichael Lynch** Creative Director **Randy Hughes** Art Director **Jason Smith** Photographer **Ron Crofoot** Copywriters **Kerry Casey** and **Mike Roe** Client **White Wave**

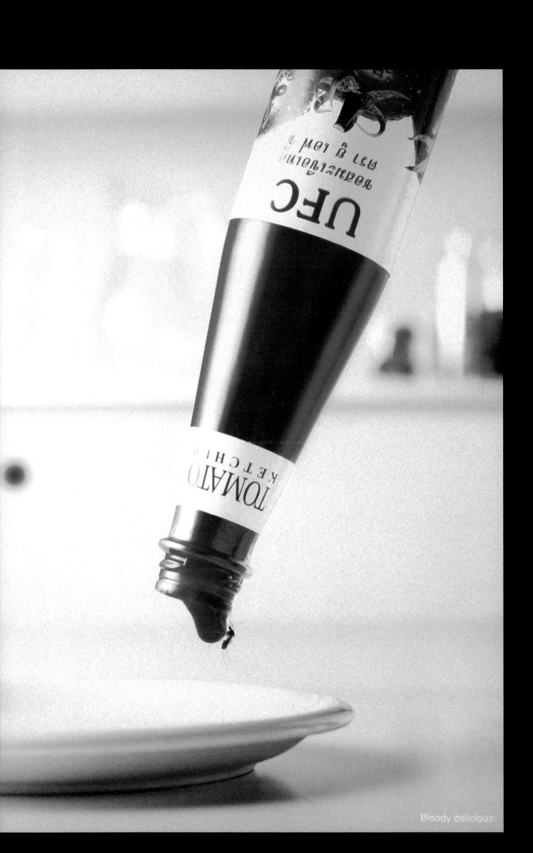

Bloody delicious

Chief Creative Officer **Thongchai Chansevikul** Photographer **ISRA** Copywriters **Vancelee Teng** and **Sirirut Angkasupornkul** Client **Universal Foods Ltd.**

Starting fires since 1868.

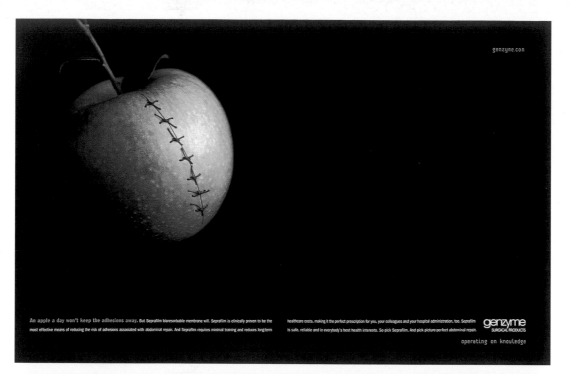

An apple a day won't keep the adhesions away. But Seprafilm bioresorbable membrane will. Seprafilm is clinically proven to be the most effective means of reducing the risk of adhesions associated with abdominal repair. And Seprafilm requires minimal training and reduces long-term healthcare costs, making it the perfect prescription for you, your colleagues and your hospital administration, too. Seprafilm is safe, reliable and in everybody's best health interests. So pick Seprafilm. And pick picture-perfect abdominal repair.

genzyme SURGICAL PRODUCTS

operating on knowledge

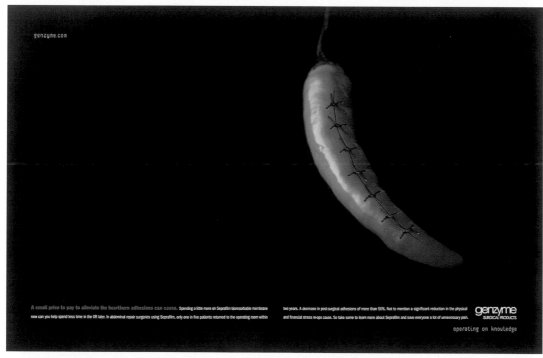

A small price to pay to alleviate the heartburn adhesions can cause. Spending a little more on Seprafilm bioresorbable membrane now can you help spend less time in the OR later. In abdominal repair surgeries using Seprafilm, only one in five patients returned to the operating room within two years. A decrease in post-surgical adhesions of more than 50%. Not to mention a significant reduction in the physical and financial stress re-ops cause. So take some to learn more about Seprafilm and save everyone a lot of unnecessary pain.

genzyme SURGICAL PRODUCTS

operating on knowledge

Life doesn't have to be a bed of adhesions. Now there's Seprafilm bioresorbable membrane. In clinical tests, Seprafilm proved to be the most effective means of reducing the risk of adhesions associated with abdominal repair. And learning to use Seprafilm requires no change to your surgical technique and only a fraction of your surgical skill, making it a product that's as convenient as it is powerful. So take some time to stop and learn more about Seprafilm. Then stop and smell what life is like when it's not full of adhesions.

genzyme SURGICAL PRODUCTS

operating on knowledge

The online clinic for mothers to be. **WebBaby**.co.uk

Imagine if the world was patterned after most health care plans.

It's a hassle having everything broken into pieces. Those of you who deal with health care plans are pretty intimate with that frustration. The problem is, most plans are a patchwork of systems, making hassles unavoidable. The only answer: a health benefits company that does things in a completely different way. One built for national employers, with centralized data, a single point of contact and one high standard nationwide. In the end, this integrated system eliminates health care frustrations. Unfortunately, problems with cross-town traffic are another story. Visit firsthealth.com/imagine or call 630.737.7078.

♥ **First Health.**
Making health care as simple as 1 2 3

Imagine if the world was patterned after most health care plans.

It's a hassle having everything broken into pieces. Those of you who deal with health care plans are pretty intimate with that frustration. The problem is, most plans are a patchwork of systems, making hassles unavoidable. The only answer: a health benefits company that does things in a completely different way. One built for national employers, with centralized data, a single point of contact and one high standard nationwide. In the end, this integrated approach eliminates health care frustrations. And makes benefits management a lot easier to swallow. Visit firsthealth.com/imagine or call 630.737.7078.

♥ **First Health.**
Making health care as simple as 1 2 3

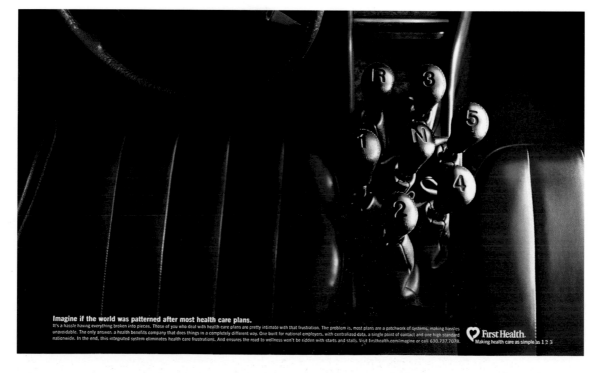

Imagine if the world was patterned after most health care plans.

It's a hassle having everything broken into pieces. Those of you who deal with health care plans are pretty intimate with that frustration. The problem is, most plans are a patchwork of systems, making hassles unavoidable. The only answer: a health benefits company that does things in a completely different way. One built for national employers, with centralized data, a single point of contact and one high standard nationwide. In the end, this integrated system eliminates health care frustrations. And ensures the road to wellness won't be ridden with starts and stalls. Visit firsthealth.com/imagine or call 630.737.7078.

♥ **First Health.**
Making health care as simple as 1 2 3

(this page) Agency **Euro RSCG Tatham** Creative Director **Jim Schmidt** Art Director **Joe Stuart** Photographer **Robert Mizono** Copywriter **Elyse Maguire** Client **First Health**

Healthcare 114, 115

ALLERGY DAY, JULY 6.

Before.

After.

Liposuction at Algoterapia Health Club Center.
Rua Visconde da Luz, 16, 1º - Cascais - phone: 01-484-2645

Agency **Edson, FCB** Creative Director **Edson Athayde** Art Director **Markus Kawamura** Copywriter **Frederico Saldanha** Client **Algoterapia Clinic**

We solve your back problems

Physiotherapy Clinic María Serrano
Velázquez, 115 · 8º Izda   Tfn. 677 531 743

keep slim. Sweeten with FINN.

keep slim. Sweeten with FINN.

keep slim. Sweeten with FINN.

ibeauty.com

Announcing a 42% increase in revenue. If you're serious about getting your products on the faces of millions each year, please call us at 212.367.7700.

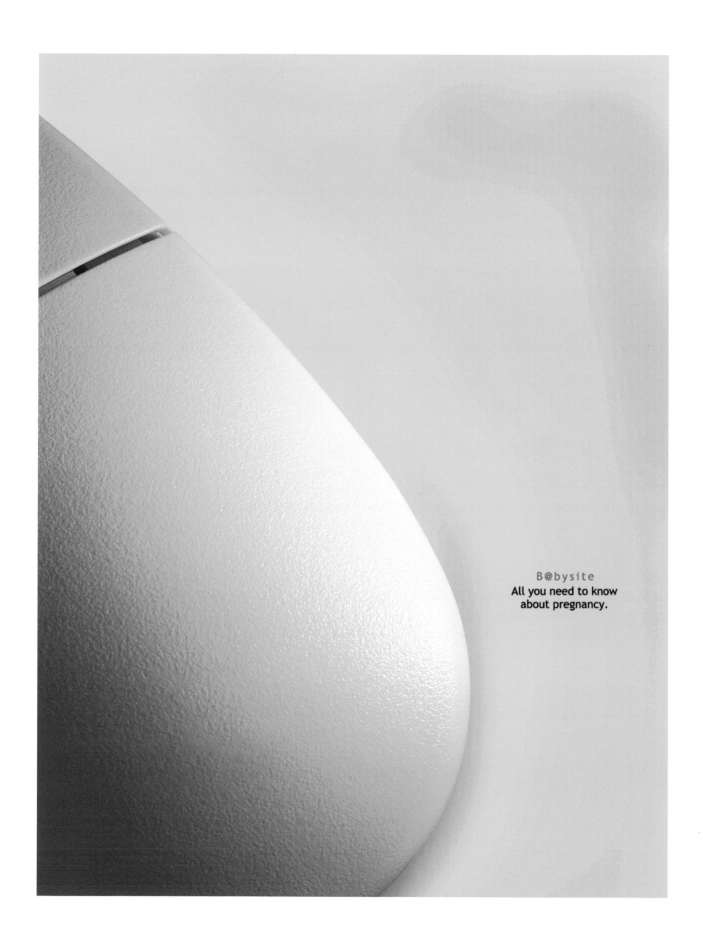

B@bysite
**All you need to know
about pregnancy.**

Agency **Edson, FCB** Creative Director **Edson Athayde** Art Director **José Carlos Silva** Copywriter **Sandro Porto** Client **Portal PT**   Internet 120,121

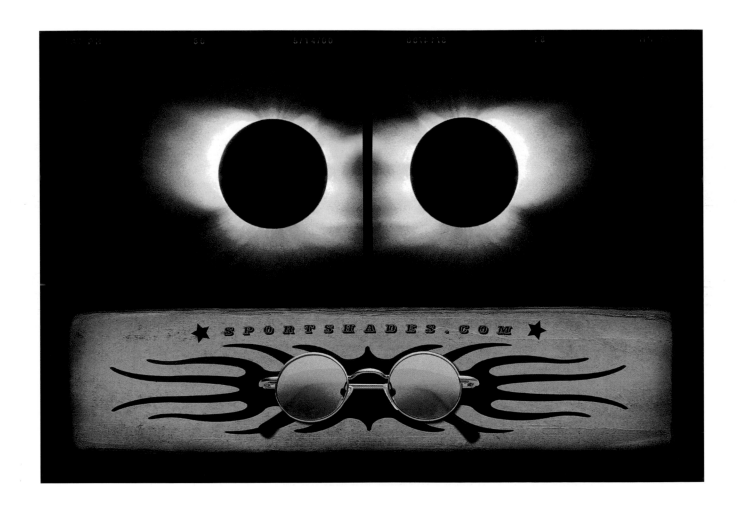

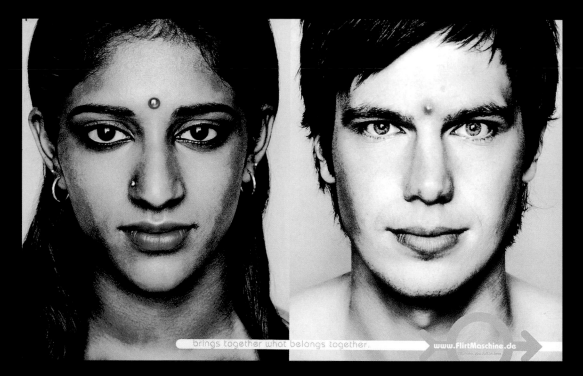

brings together what belongs together.   www.FlirtMaschine.de

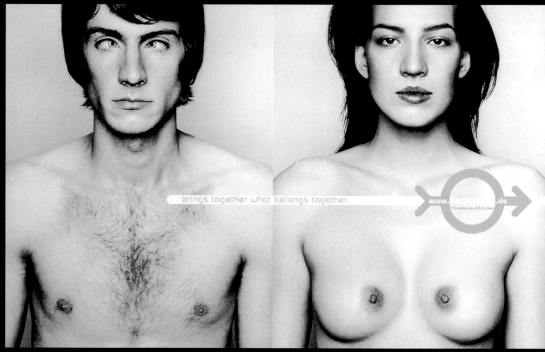

brings together what belongs together.   www.FlirtMaschine.de

brings together what belongs together.   www.FlirtMaschine.de

(page) Agency **Jung von Matt Werbeagentur GmbH** Creative Directors **Goetz Ulmer** and **Thomas Wildberger** Art Director **Corinna Falusi** Photographer **Billy & Hells** Copywriter **Gunnar Roeser** Client **PopNet Agentscape AG** Internet 122, 123

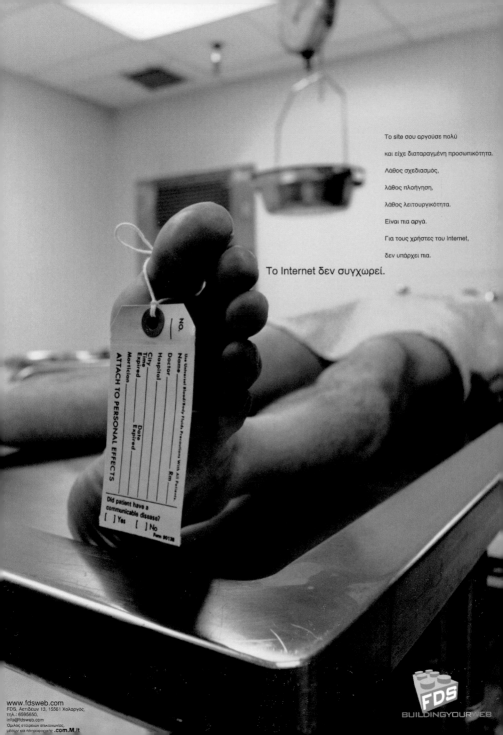

Το site σου αργούσε πολύ

και είχε διαταραγμένη προσωπικότητα.

Λάθος σχεδιασμός,

λάθος πλοήγηση,

λάθος λειτουργικότητα.

Είναι πια αργά.

Για τους χρήστες του Internet,

δεν υπάρχει πια.

Το Internet δεν συγχωρεί.

www.fdsweb.com
FDS, Αετιδέων 13, 15561 Χολαργός,
τηλ.: 6595650,
info@fdsweb.com
Όμιλος εταιρειών επικοινωνίας,
μέλων και πληροφορικής .com.M.lt

To Internet δεν συγχωρεί.

Σου σέρβιραν
ό,τι ήθελαν!
Και το site σου
το πλήρωσε με τη ζωή του.
Αυτά παθαίνει
όταν έχει λάθος σχεδιασμό,
λάθος περιεχόμενο
και λάθος λειτουργικότητα.
Λυπάμαι που στο λέω,
αλλά για τους χρήστες του Internet,
είναι απλά νεκρό.

www.fdsweb.com
FDS, Αετιδέων 13, 15561 Χολαργός,
τηλ.: 6595650,
info@fdsweb.com
Όμιλος εταιρειών επικοινωνίας .com.M.it

FDS
BUILDINGYOURWEB

Was immer Sie empfangen möchten, geniessen Sie's bei Ihnen zu Hause. Details zu digitalem Fernsehen und Radio, hispeed*-Internet via Kabelanschluss und was die Zukunft sonst noch bringt, gibts unter 0844 80 40 10 oder www.cablecom.ch

CABLECOM
DIE GANZE WELT ZU HAUSE

Was immer Sie empfangen möchten, geniessen Sie's bei Ihnen zu Hause. Details zu digitalem Fernsehen und Radio, hispeed*-Internet via Kabelanschluss und was die Zukunft sonst noch bringt, gibts unter 0844 80 40 10 oder www.cablecom.ch

CABLECOM
DIE GANZE WELT ZU HAUSE

Was immer Sie empfangen möchten, geniessen Sie's bei Ihnen zu Hause. Details zu digitalem Fernsehen und Radio, hispeed*-Internet via Kabelanschluss und was die Zukunft sonst noch bringt, gibts unter 0844 80 40 10 oder www.cablecom.ch

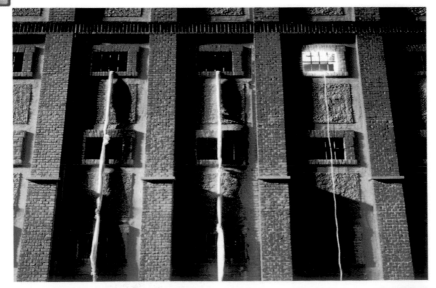

CABLECOM
DIE GANZE WELT ZU HAUSE

(this page) Agency **Jean et Moutmarin** Creative Director **Gerard Jean** Art Director **Thierry Meunier** Photographer **Richard Dangerfield** Copywriter **Christopher Trouvé-Dugény** Client **houra Fr** Internet 126, 127

INSIDE EVERY MAN THERE'S A FAT BOY TRYING TO GET OUT.

It's in you, all right. A Fat Boy? Or a Sportster® or Wide Glide® or Road King? Chromed steel and perfect paint and when you hit the starter it takes you into the wind where it's all good. Well, don't let too much more life slip by before you let it out. In this world, time you miss is time you don't get back. 1-800-443-2153 or www.harley-davidson.com. The Legend Rolls On.™

Peter Fonda rides a 2000 Chief.™

SINCE 1901

Indian™

AMERICA'S FIRST MOTORCYCLE

THE LEGEND LIVES

AMERICAN MADE · GILROY CALIFORNIA © 2000 INDIAN MOTORCYCLE

MADE BY HAND. BUILT BY HEART. FOR THE DEALER NEAREST YOU: INDIANMOTORCYCLE.COM

INDIAN MOTORCYCLE ENCOURAGES YOU TO WEAR A HELMET, EYE PROTECTION AND APPROPRIATE RIDING APPAREL. DO NOT DRINK AND RIDE. IT GIVES MOTORCYCLING A BAD NAME. INDIAN HIGHLY RECOMMENDS THE MOTORCYCLE SAFETY FOUNDATION RIDER COURSE. IT WORKS. FOR MORE INFORMATION CALL MSF TOLL FREE 1.800.446.9227.

His hair shows he's been dreaming of the NX4 Falcon.

Introducing the NX4 Falcon.
The 400cc of your dreams.

They're dreaming of the new NX4 Falcon.

Introducing the NX4 Falcon.
The 400cc of your dreams.

Another biker who dreamed of the NX4 Falcon all night long.

Introducing the NX4 Falcon.
The 400cc of your dreams.

Agency **DM9 DDB** Creative Directors **Erh Ray, Sergio Valente** and **Camila Franco** Art Director **Pedro Cappeletti** Photographers **Richard Kohout** and **Arnaldo Pappalardo** Copywriter **Jáder Rossetto** Client **Moto Honda da Amazônia** Motorcycles 130, 131

Buell
DIFFERENT IN EVERY SENSE®

Cyclone™ M2 shown in Blue Streak. Demo ride a Buell. Call 1-800-490-9635 for the dealer nearest you. www.buell.com

©2000 Buell Distribution Corp.

Torquey V-Twin | 85 ft. lbs. @ 4900rpm | Arm-jerking Acceleration | Off-the-line Muscle | Free Alterations

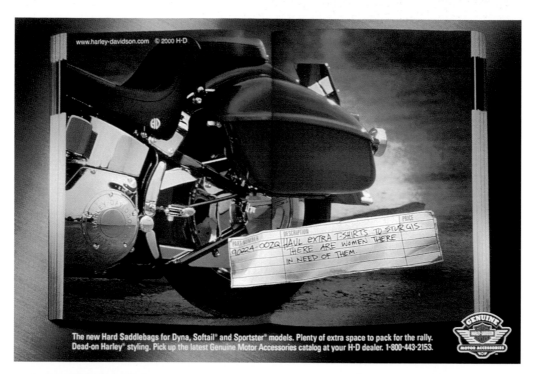

The new Hard Saddlebags for Dyna, Softail® and Sportster® models. Plenty of extra space to pack for the rally. Dead-on Harley® styling. Pick up the latest Genuine Motor Accessories catalog at your H-D dealer. 1-800-443-2153.

The Low-Profile Smoked Windshield. Custom fit and function from the same people who designed your Harley.® See the full line of windshields in the latest Genuine Motor Accessories catalog. Call 1-800-443-2153 for directions to an H-D dealer.

Shotgun-Style Slip-On Mufflers. Rediscover why nothing else on earth sounds like a Harley.® See the full line of custom pipes in the latest Genuine Motor Accessories catalog at your H-D dealer. Call 1-800-443-2153 for directions.

Agency **Carmichael Lynch** Creative Director **Jim Nelson** Art Director **Hans Hansen** Photographers **Joe Paczkowski** and **Madison Ford** Copywriter **Eric Sorensen** Client **Harley Davidson**   Motorcycles 132, 133

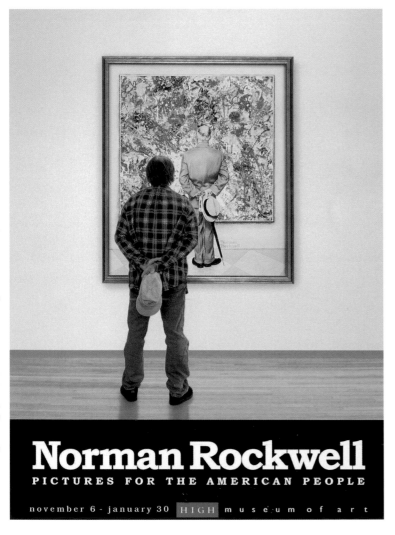

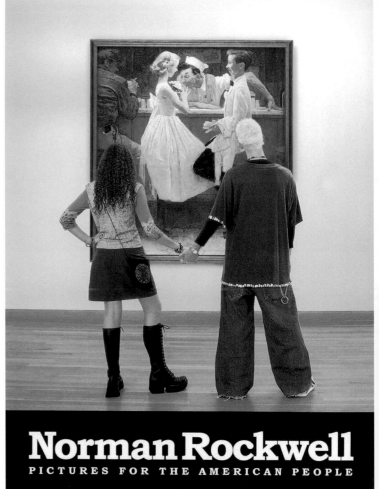

(this spread) Agency **BaylessCronin** Creative Director **Jerry Cronin** Art Director **Laura Briney** Photographer **Jim Fiscus** Client **High Museum of Art**

fig. 1

fig. 2

THE EXHIBIT. *The Muhammad Ali Center. Opening Soon.*

Send your donation to The Muhammad Ali Center, One Riverfront Plaza, Suite 1702, Louisville, KY 40202.

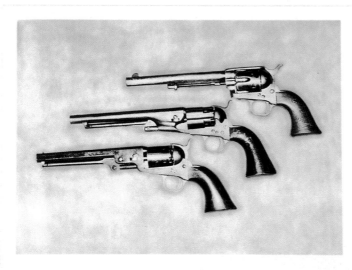

It's a lot like collecting stamps, only nobody makes fun of you.

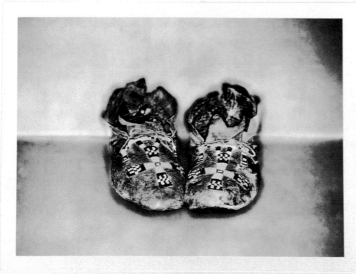

From a time when cross-training meant chasing down dinner and slitting its throat.

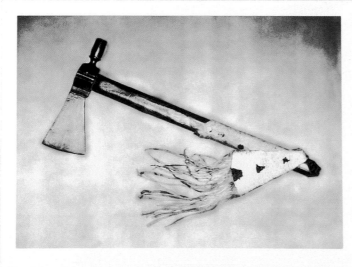

Look at it as a way to safeguard the rest of your collection.

BACK HOME IN TUMBLETON, ALABAMA, PETE PETERSON LIVED FOR HIS TEAM. SOMEWHERE IN THE SOUTH PACIFIC, HE DIED FOR ONE TOO.

His real name was Lemuel Byrd Peterson, but like all the boys in the Peterson family, he wound up with the nickname of "Pete." He had blonde hair and blue eyes, and those who knew him say he was one heck of a basketball player who would do anything for his team. He was born in 1918, and like lots of others in South Alabama, his father was a sharecropper who raised cotton and peanuts on his land.

Though farm life could be tough, Pete loved being outdoors and he never missed a chance to hunt, fish or play ball. And while he enjoyed farming, Pete's career plans were quite different from his father's, as what he truly loved to do was work on cars. They say it was pretty darn rare to find Pete Peterson without a little grease on his hands. Eventually he landed a job as the mechanic at Shelby's Service Station. It was there he met a girl he would later marry, Nina.

When the war began heating up in 1941, so did work around South Alabama. Nina took a job at a sawmill and Pete's parents began logging 16-hour days in a sock factory. But Pete felt his contribution to the war should be made far away from his home. So he enlisted in the Army Air Corps and was assigned to be a tailgunner for a B29 fighter plane called "The Ghastly Goose." The crew of the Goose was a tight knit team who became known as a highly effective force in the missions they flew over Japan. But in January 1945, when anit-aircraft fire struck her fuel tanks, the Goose was forced to crash land in the Pacific. All 12 members of the crew survived and climbed atop the plane, which they knew could float for up to 48 hours, to await rescue. Shortly before dusk, they were spotted by another plane which signaled that, because it was getting dark, pick up would have to wait until morning. It was the last time anyone ever saw Pete Peterson and the crew of the Ghastly Goose. When rescuers came at dawn, they had vanished. To this day, no one knows what happened. In keeping with MIA policy at the time, Pete and all the others were declared dead a year and a day later.

They say that, even though they never made it home, the bombing missions Pete and his crew flew over Japan were instrumental in winning the war. And that's just kind of fitting, because Pete Peterson of Tumbleton, Alabama always was one heck of a good guy to have on your team.

JOIN US IN REMEMBERING THE OVER 8,000 ALABAMIANS WHO HAVE DIED FOR THIS COUNTRY. VISIT THE ALABAMA VETERANS MEMORIAL AT 459 AND LIBERTY PARKWAY.

ALABAMA VETERANS MEMORIAL

IT WAS SO HOT IN THE PHILIPPINES THE DAY EARL BRAKE CELEBRATED HIS 21ST BIRTHDAY, HE THOUGHT HE WAS GOING TO DIE. SEVEN DAYS LATER, HE DID.

In a letter he sent home the day he turned 21, Earl Brake wrote, "I'm trying to keep a smile on my face even though it was so hot here today I thought I was going to die." Truth was, they say Earl Brake could've grinned 24 hours a day. The youngest boy in a family of five children, Earl was always the most fun loving. He had wavy blonde hair and bright green eyes, and his favorite word was "dadgummit." To good old Earl, everything was always "dadgummit." He grew-up in the little burg of Watson, Alabama during the depression. But Earl was always known as the kind of fellow who wouldn't let anyone around him get depressed. He had a sister named Helen and brothers known by nicknames like Doodle, Red and Keg. Most of the family worked in the coal mines, but Earl's father wanted better for his boys so he opened a small grocery store there in town. All of his boys worked for him.

When they weren't working, the Brake boys would head to the swimming hole or walk the two miles to the movies over in Brookside. It was a great place to be a boy.

But like all of his older brothers, Earl was forced to grow-up early when he was drafted into the Army in the summer of 1943. After basic training, Earl joined thousands of other boys in the jungles of the Philippines. While there, Earl quickly earned a reputation for being as good with a Browning automatic rifle as he was at telling a joke.

One day, heavy fighting broke out on the island and Earl's platoon found out that a Japanese force three times the size of their own was about to overrun them. The only way they could escape would be if someone climbed to a hilltop and put down cover fire to hold off the Japanese long enough for the rest of the platoon to move out. The sergeant asked for a volunteer and, because he was the only one who wasn't married, Earl volunteered. The next thing you know, Earl Brake was on top of the hill giving 'em hell.

Because of him, his buddies made it out of there. Earl wasn't so lucky. He died there, alone in the jungle a million miles away from home. It was just 7 days after he and some of the guys had drunk a toast to celebrate his 21st birthday. It only takes one bullet to kill a man, and Earl was shot more than 100 times.

Sometime later a letter arrived at the Brake household. Well after all three of Earl's older brothers had made it back from the war alive. The letter from a buddy said, "Sometimes I dream and I see Earl walking back toward me with that big smile of his. It's a shame men like Earl have to die so that the rest of us can enjoy freedom." His big brother recalls, "I always took up for him in a fight. I wish'd I could've been there that day."

For his bravery, Earl was never awarded the Congressional Medal of Honor. But that doesn't matter because the men whose lives he saved that day, many years ago, would be all too happy to tell you that good old Earl Brake from Watson, Alabama was a hero, alright.

And dadgummit that's the truth.

JOIN US IN REMEMBERING THE OVER 8,000 ALABAMIANS WHO HAVE DIED FOR THIS COUNTRY. VISIT THE ALABAMA VETERANS MEMORIAL AT 459 AND LIBERTY PARKWAY.

ALABAMA VETERANS MEMORIAL

THESE DAYS A TRIP OVERSEAS COSTS ABOUT $900, BUT IN 1944, TWENTY-FIVE YEAR OLD NEAL SNELL OF ASBURY, ALABAMA PAID A CONSIDERABLY HIGHER PRICE.

Picture if you will a real Coca-Cola truck rumbling along a gravel road on a hot South Alabama morning not really so long ago. In the little town of Asbury, everybody knew everybody and everybody knew 25 year old Neal Snell. He was the Coca-Cola man. He was married to a sweetheart of a woman named Beth, and they had a beautiful little girl with a curly Shirley Temple mane named Theresa. It was 1943 and WWII was something townsfolk and the rest of the world lived and died for every day. As a boy, Neal dreamed of being a pilot. Years later, in a box hidden away in an attic, there are still-filled notebooks with drawings of planes. One summer he even took flying lessons. Secret flying lessons which he kept secret until one day his parents came to an airfield where Neal's cousin was waiting. "Where is Neal?" they asked. The cousin pointed toward a small plane in the wild blue yonder and said, "He's up there. He's up there!"

When he was drafted into the United States Marines in 1943, he probably thought it wasn't quite fair that he couldn't go into the Army Air Force. But he complained to no one. After basic training, his young wife and daughter moved to a tiny apartment to live with him in Laguna Beach, California. Together they swam in the ocean and built sandcastles and had a birthday party for their three year old daughter, Theresa. For the little family from Alabama, it was like a vacation. But like all vacations, it had to end. And it did when Neal got his orders. He was being sent to Hawaii to await transfer to another island. An island called Iwo Jima.

They said their goodbyes, and mother and daughter drove back to Alabama.

The telegram came on a beautiful, sunny Alabama afternoon. The Western Union man had the unbearable task of taking it to the family. He took it to Neal's father who was working at the hardware store in Asbury. He was devastated. A little while later, Neal's father and other family members took the short drive out to Neal's house to tell the horrible news to his young wife and daughter. His daughter, Theresa, still barely remembers that day. "Mother was in the kitchen making fudge when the car came up the driveway. She knew why they were there and she fell apart. A little while later, she took me out on the porch and the two of us just sat out there. Just us. We were alone."

Next time you hear the National Anthem or look up at our flag flying high in the air, look at the colors and the stars and remember the young man who drove the Coca-Cola truck and worried about his wife and daughter. He is up there.

JOIN US IN REMEMBERING THE OVER 8,000 ALABAMIANS WHO HAVE DIED FOR THIS COUNTRY. VISIT THE ALABAMA VETERANS MEMORIAL AT 459 AND LIBERTY PARKWAY.

ALABAMA VETERANS MEMORIAL

**Star Trek at the
Science Museum**

Exhibition:
15.06.00–22.04.01

Booking line:
0870 870 4856

Agency **TBWA/London** Creative Director **Trevor Beattie** Art Director **Paul Belford** Photographer **Laurie Haskell** Copywriter **Nigel Roberts** Client **The Science Museum**   Museums 138, 139

WHAT PEOPLE STARED AT BEFORE MTV.

Visit us at www.eisnermuseum.org. Museum Hours: Tues.-Sat. 11-5.

EISNER MUSEUM of advertising and design

SIDE 1

1. ALBUM COVERS.
Years ago, they captivated music lovers.
2. MANY WERE A CANVAS
for artistic expression and storytelling.
3. THEY EVEN CHANGED
the way records were sold and remembered.
4. SEE THE ORIGINAL ART
form featuring the best of jazz and rock.

William F. Eisner Museum of Advertising & Design. A component of the Milwaukee Institute of Art & Design.

THE ART OF THE ALBUM COVER. OPENS MARCH 9, 2001. CALL 414.203.0371.
208 NORTH WATER STREET, MILWAUKEE, WISCONSIN.

This Time See Them Without The Black Light And Incense.

1. Album Covers.
In 1939 they underwent a design revolution.
2. By The '60s & '70s
many reflected the turbulence of the times.
3. Visually Arresting,
they heightened the sensory experience.
4. Treat Your Eyes
to 4 decades of eclectic pop culture images.

1

SHOW ONLY
WWW.EISNER MUSEUM.ORG

William F. Eisner Museum of Advertising & Design. A component of the Milwaukee Institute of Art & Design. Museum Hours: Tues.-Sat. 11-5.

EISNER MUSEUM of advertising and design

THE ART OF THE ALBUM COVER. OPENS MARCH 9, 2001. CALL 414.203.0371.
208 NORTH WATER STREET, MILWAUKEE, WISCONSIN.

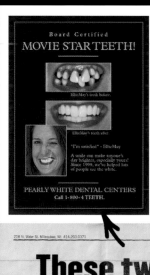

Board Certified
MOVIE STAR TEETH!

EllieMay's teeth before.

EllieMay's teeth after.

"I'm satisfied" - EllieMay

A smile can make anyone's day brighter, especially yours! Since 1999, we've helped lots of people see the white.

PEARLY WHITE DENTAL CENTERS
Call 1-800- 4 TEETH.

THE NEWTON ABBY MINT PRESENTS

The Bigfoot
COMMEMORATIVE PLATE

BIGFOOT
2000

Now you can cherish the spirit of Bigfoot everyday with our limited-issue hand-painted porcelain china heirloom.

To order this elegant collectable at the issue price of just
$79.99 - with our 365-day guarantee - call 1-800-PLATES

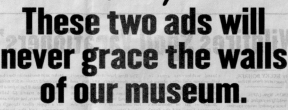

208 N. Water St, Milwaukee, WI 414.203.0371   A component of the Milwaukee Institute of Art & Design

These two ads will never grace the walls of our museum.

Unless, of course, we decide to do an exhibit devoted to crap.

THE FACTS
■ Gallery Night Opening
Friday, October 20th, 6-9p.m.
■ Grand Opening Saturday,
October 21st, 11a.m.-3p.m.
■ Hours Tuesday-Saturday
11a.m.-5p.m.
Located on the corner of North Water and Chicago Streets

The William F. Eisner Museum of
Advertising & Design Grand
Opening October 20th and 21st.
FREE ADMISSION
October 20th and 21st

While most people think that the majority of advertising

belongs on the bottom of a bird cage, we believe it sometimes belongs on the walls of our museum. That is, if it holds up to our standards. Visitors here can enjoy some of the world's best ads. And depending on how successful we are in getting the word

out, this ad may one day be showcased in there as well.

EISNER MUSEUM of advertising and design
Please see www.eisnermuseum.org for upcoming events.

WE'D LIKE TO THANK ALL THE LITTLE PEOPLE FOR HELPING MAKE THIS MUSEUM POSSIBLE.

Being the only museum of its kind, it's soon to become an icon, too.

EISNER MUSEUM of advertising and design

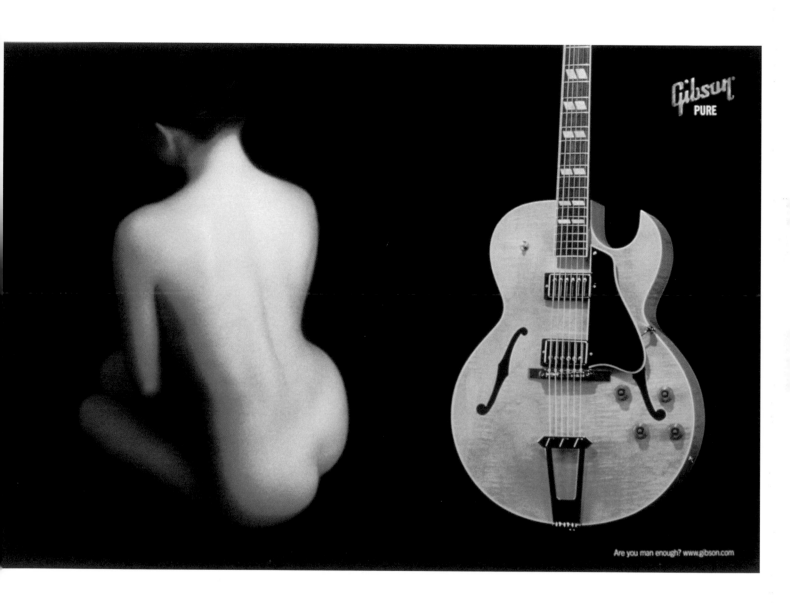

ELECTRONIC FILE TRANSFER
plotting your course
3

NEW TECHNOLOGIES AND THE INCREASING SPEED of business are demanding fast file delivery and high-speed connectivity. The Internet has become the vehicle of choice, and companies that market file transfer technology are helping designers and production people navigate the workflow maze. Internet-based graphic arts applications help streamline the process, improve communication, and promote online collaboration with applications like preflighting, digital asset management, and remote and soft proofing. Files are moving more quickly and more accurately. Maintenance of color integrity in the digital world means production and creative people can review images and manage work together, no matter where in the world they are located.

SCANNING
in the future, will the world be flat?
1

THE WORLD OF SCANNING USED TO BE ROUND. Common wisdom held that drum scanners were the only way to get accurate scans. While it's still true that the best drum technology provides superior shadow detail and resolution, as well as color fidelity and overall quality, the world is changing dimension as flatbed scanners improve. The evolution of CCD, or charge-coupled device technology, the inclusion of color management features, fast batch scanning, single-pass scanning technology, lower cost, and easy operation are converting many people to the Flat Scanning Society. The world of image capture also is being invaded by digital cameras. Recent sightings include a new 6.6 megapixel CMOS sensor that allows full-size, high-resolution images to be captured using standard 35mm lenses. This technology, while still no match for the color fidelity of film and scanning, eventually could transform the future of high-quality imaging.

PROOFING
look again
4

WHEN IS A PROOF NOT A PROOF? In the pre-digital world, proofs were either actual press proofs or film-based, with halftone dots. Today, continuous-tone, dot-less digital proofs are just as likely to be called a contract proof. Commercial printers and prepress shops often use more than one type of proofer, and each one offers a facsimile of varying closeness to what real ink on real paper may end up looking like. Today's proofing options include high-performance ink-jet systems, full-format proofs often known as digital bluelines, dye-sublimation printers, and digital halftone proofers, which typically use a common RIP to image both the digital halftone proof and the plate, giving a higher degree of dot-to-dot fidelity. In this increasingly digital world, it is critical to ask questions so that limitations and expectations are clear, and adjustments that may be necessary on press can be anticipated.

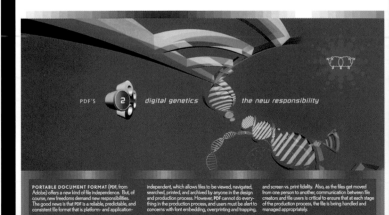

PDF'S
digital genetics   *the new responsibility*
2

PORTABLE DOCUMENT FORMAT (PDF, from Adobe) offers a new kind of file independence. But, of course, new freedoms demand new responsibilities. The good news is that PDF is a reliable, predictable, and consistent file format that is platform- and application-independent, which allows files to be viewed, navigated, searched, printed, and archived by anyone in the design and production process. However, PDF cannot do everything in the production process, and users must be alert to concerns with font embedding, overprinting and trapping, and screen vs. print fidelity. Also, as the files get moved from one person to another, communication between file creators and file users is critical to ensure that at each stage of the production process, the file is being handled and managed appropriately.

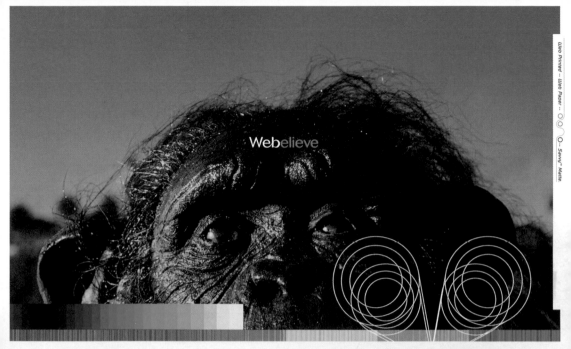

Webelieve

Champion Web.

The evolution
of web paper communications through human digital connections.

N2 Savvy™ Matte

Champion Web.™

009061

3:00 PM

3:13 PM

Brave Soldier Wound Healing Ointment. It soothes pain, speeds healing and reduces scarring. It works good. To order call 888-711-BRAV. www.bravesoldier.com

8:12 AM

8:30 AM

Brave Soldier Wound Healing Ointment. It soothes pain, speeds healing and reduces scarring. It works good. To order call 888-711-BRAV. www.bravesoldier.com

6:40 am

6:53 am

Brave Soldier Wound Healing Ointment. It soothes pain, speeds healing and reduces scarring. It works good. To order call 888-711-BRAV. www.bravesoldier.com

(this page) Agency **Stewart Zimmerman** Creative Director **Pat Zimmerman** and **Rob Stewart** Art Director **Pat Zimmerman** Photographer **Chris Wimpey** Illustrators (top and bottom) **Charlie Haygood** (middle) **Gordon Morris** and **Charlie Haygood** Copywriter **Rob Stewart** Client

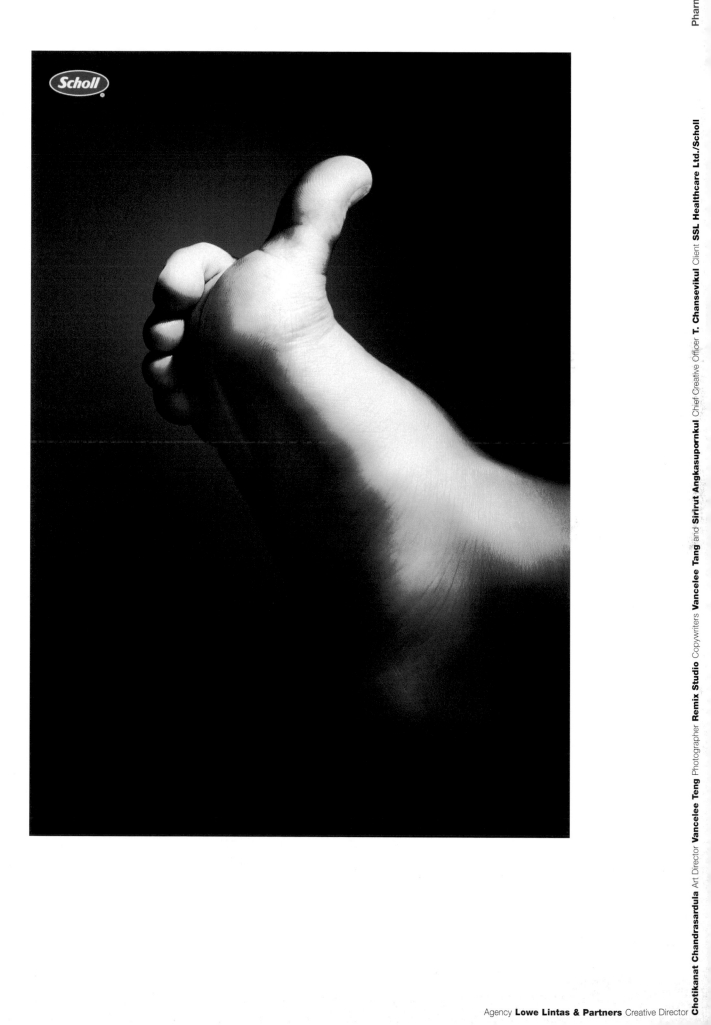

Pharmaceutical 146,147

SSL Healthcare Ltd./Scholl

Chief Creative Officer T. Chansevikul Client

Copywriters Vancelee Teng and Sirirut Angkasupornkul

Photographer Remix Studio

Chotikanat Chandrasardula Art Director Vancelee Teng

Agency Lowe Lintas & Partners Creative Director

ANTI-ITCH FORMULA.

(this page) **Agency Ammirati Paris** Creative Director **Doug Robinson** Art Director and Designer **Deborah Prenger** Photographer **Ron Baxter Smith** Copywriter **Tom Goudie** Client **Novartis Consumers Health Canada**   **Pharmaceutical** 148,149

太宁前　　　　太宁后

太宁.有效保护痔粘膜

You'll think twice about putting your feet on it. Not to mention your stapler and your pen.

Just remember to flip it over if your family stops by.

Don't worry, after time you'll even be able to put your coffee cup on it.

Euro RSCG Tatham Creative Director Jim Schmidt Art Director Joe Stuart Photographer Mark Laita Copywriter Elyse Maguire Client Bretford Furniture

(this page) Agency Pharmaceutical/Products 152,153

beautiful

soft

www.berkshireblanket.com

www.berkshireblanket.com

Berkshire Blanket®
Premium Quality

Berkshire Blanket®
Premium Quality

Berkshire Blanket®
Premium Quality

OF ALL
THE THINGS
THAT CAN
RUIN A
FISHERMAN'S
MORNING,
OUR LINE WILL
NEVER BE ONE OF
THEM.

TOUGH

Rapala

WHAT
SEPARATES
GOOD
FISHERMEN
FROM
THE GREAT?
ABOUT 1/1000th
OF AN INCH.

FINESSE

Rapala

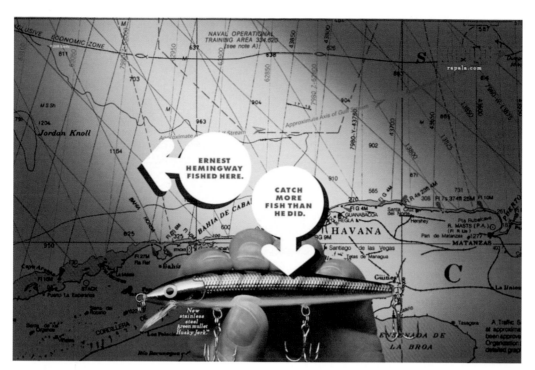

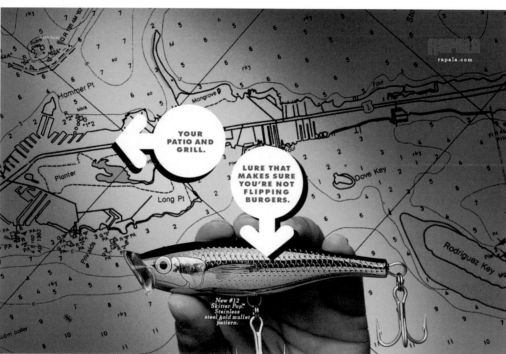

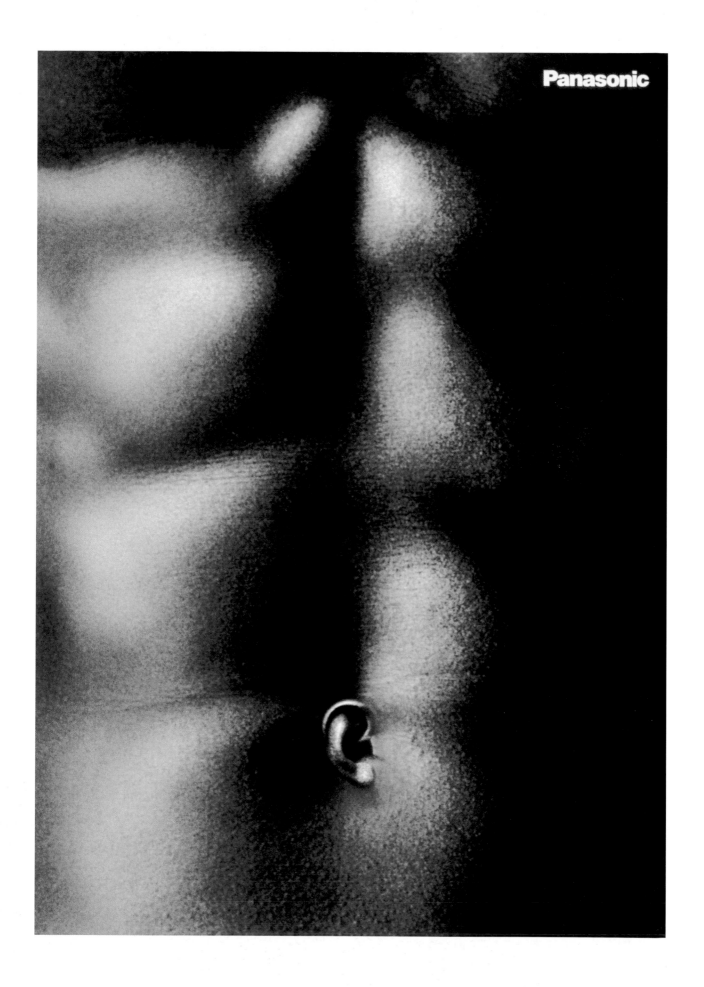

Agency **Jung Von Matt/Limmat AG** Creative Director **Daniel Meier** Client **John Jay Electronics**

UNITED STATES DEPARTMENT OF HOUSING SELECT CUTS

☙ TERMITES EAT HOUSES ☙

Ignoring this fact will not make it go away. Spectracide Terminate do-it-yourself termite stakes. When used as directed, it effectively kills subterranean termites in the ground where they live. And in the battle against termites, if you're not doing everything you can, then you're not doing enough. Retailers are standing by.

— **DO SOMETHING. DO IT NOW.** —

☙ TERMITES EAT HOUSES ☙

Ignoring this fact will not make it go away. Spectracide Terminate do-it-yourself termite stakes. When used as directed, it effectively kills subterranean termites in the ground where they live. And in the battle against termites, if you're not doing everything you can, then you're not doing enough. Retailers are standing by.

— **DO SOMETHING. DO IT NOW.** —

PUT THESE GLASSES ON AND YOU'LL SEE WHAT RAID DOES TO THE INSECTS IN YOUR HOME.

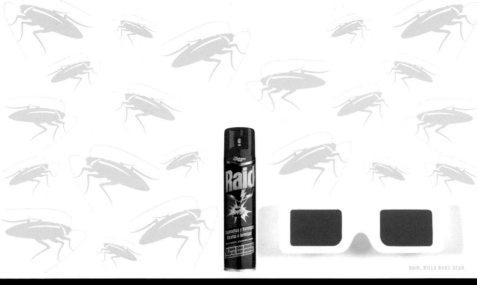

RAID. KILLS BUGS DEAD.

Raid. The bug hunter.

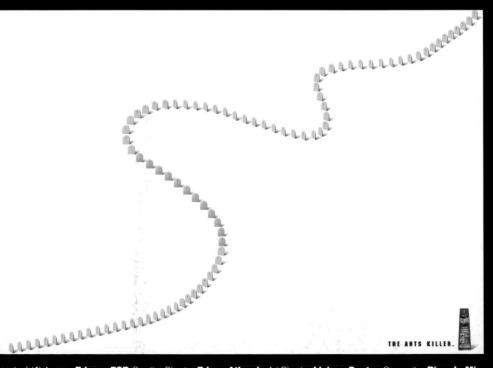

THE ANTS KILLER.

Create your own drive-in theater.
Park.

Cars have lots of features. Some even have a double feature. Introducing the new Jensen mobile video systems. With Jensen titanium plated speakers, it's a veritable entertainment center on four wheels. For more information on our full line of car audio and video equipment, call 1(877) JENSEN-0.

JENSEN
www.jensenaudio.com

Airport Diorama for Burbank airport. This document is 1/4 size. Live area is 61" x 42". Add appropriate bleed.

Leave the world and the wire behind.

JENSEN
www.jensen.com

Jensen wireless headphones and speakers let you listen to what you want.
When you want. Wherever you want. Remember, reality exists between your ears, wherever they may be.
For more information on our full line of wireless audio products, visit our website or call 1(800)732-6866.

Super Strong Industrial Threads

Products 164, 165

Client Arno Copywriter Carlos Fonseca Art Director Luis Tastaldi Photographer Valentim Fialdini Creative Directors Tião Bernardi, J.R. D'Elboux and Rita Corradi Agency Young & Rubicam Brasil (this page)

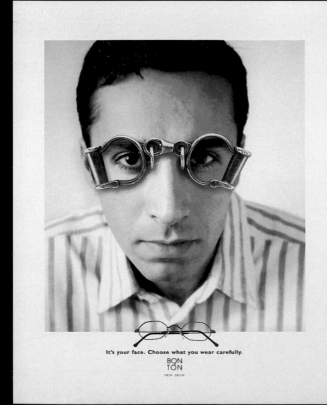

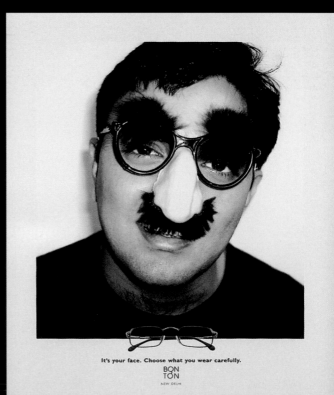

It's your face. Choose what you wear carefully.

BON
TON

NEW DELHI

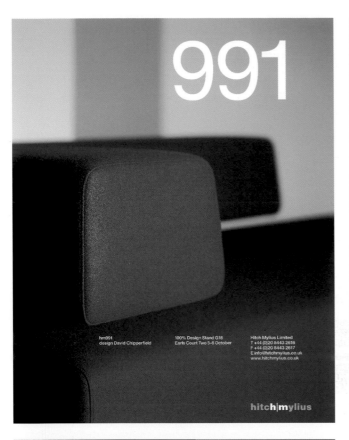

991

hm991
design David Chipperfield

100% Design Stand G16
Earls Court Two 5–6 October

Hitch Mylius Limited
T +44 (0)20 8443 2616
F +44 (0)20 8443 2617
E info@hitchmylius.co.uk
www.hitchmylius.co.uk

hitch|mylius

hm992
design David Chipperfield

Hitch Mylius Limited
T +44 (0)20 8443 2616
F +44 (0)20 8443 2617
E info@hitchmylius.co.uk
www.hitchmylius.co.uk

992

hitch|mylius

hm61
design Nigel Coates

Hitch Mylius Limited
T +44 (0)20 8443 2616
F +44 (0)20 8443 2617
E info@hitchmylius.co.uk
www.hitchmylius.co.uk

61

h|m

hm29
contract and domestic
seating collection

Hitch Mylius Limited
T +44 (0)20 8443 2616
F +44 (0)20 8443 2617
E info@hitchmylius.co.uk
www.hitchmylius.co.uk

29

hitch|mylius

THERE'S FULL MOONLIGHT 12 TIMES A YEAR.

THAT LEAVES JUST 353 NIGHTS.

BEGA is a specialist for luminaires used in and on buildings, in gardens and streets. A partner for all lighting planners and designers who create architecture with light.

BEGA

NOT EVERYTHING THAT GLOWS
LOOKS THAT GOOD BY DAY.

SOME THINGS DO.

BEGA is a specialist for luminaires used in and on buildings, in gardens and streets. A partner for all lighting planners and designers who create architecture with light.

BEGA

EUROPE HAS 4,380 HOURS OF
NIGHT EVERY YEAR.

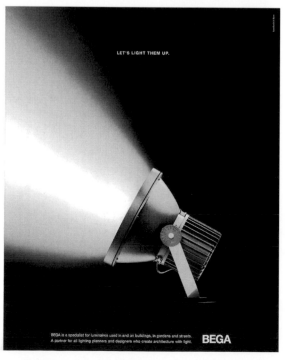

LET'S LIGHT THEM UP.

BEGA is a specialist for luminaires used in and on buildings, in gardens and streets. A partner for all lighting planners and designers who create architecture with light.

BEGA

(this page) Agency **Leonhardt & Kern Werbung GmbH** Creative Director **Waldemar Meister** Art Director **Jonas Ruch** Photographers **Paavo Ruch** and **Rolf Herkner** Copywriter **Philipp Heimsch** Client **BEGA Gantenbrink-Leuchten KG**   Products 168, 169

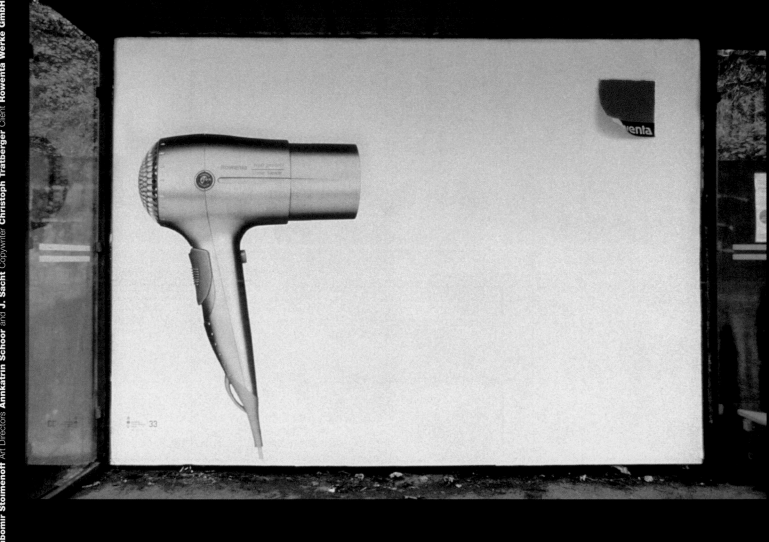

Scottex Toillet Papper. As soft as your skin.

Scottex

Edson, FCB Creative Director Edson Athayde Art Director Pedro Mabalhaes Copywriter Mauricio Machado Client Scootex

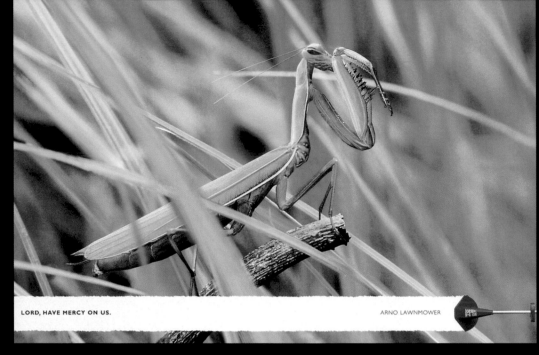

LORD, HAVE MERCY ON US.　　　　　ARNO LAWNMOWER

KEEP OFF GRASS.　　　　　ARNO LAWNMOWER

KEEP OFF GRASS.　　　　　ARNO LAWNMOWER

breathe

passion

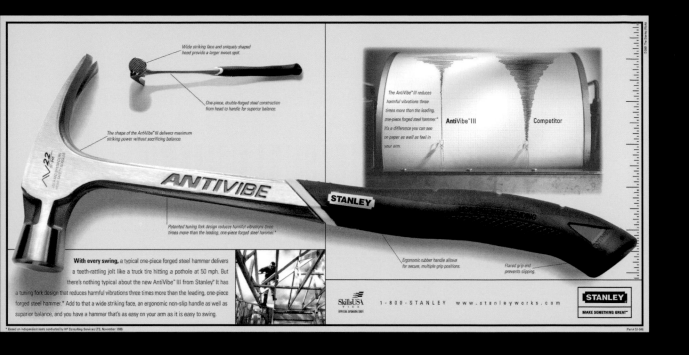
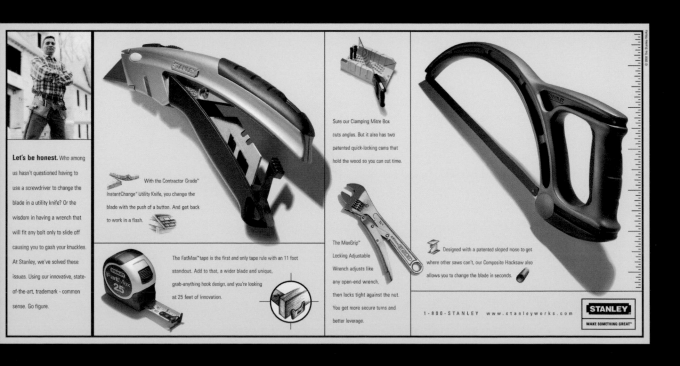

0 74300 00933 9

EINSTEIN: MODEL TRAINS.
GANDHI: MODEL TRAINS.
HITLER: NO MODEL TRAINS.

RELIVE THE JOYS
OF CHILDHOOD.

WITHOUT THE
BEDWETTING PART.

FOR ONCE IN YOUR SAD,
WORMLIKE EXISTENCE,
EVERYONE HAS TO LOOK
UP TO YOU.

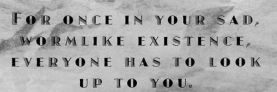

NEED BETTER SECURITY?

GET THE ARMY ON YOUR SIDE.

NEED BETTER SECURITY?

GET THE ARMY ON YOUR SIDE.

NEED BETTER SECURITY?

GET THE ARMY ON YOUR SIDE.

bimba
furniture restoration

Young & Rubicam Creative Director **Arturo López** Art Director **Ana Serrano** Photographer **Angel Alvarez** Copywriter **Raquel Diez** Client **Bimba**

Imagine.

Hairstylist. Seefeldstrasse 182, 8008 Zürich, Telefon 01 422 42 42

Zelo
Hairstylist

Case Closed.

Close your lens case and open your eyes to the methods and benefits of the revolutionary Excimer Laser Refractive Surgery (PRK and LASIK) procedure.

**REFRACTIVE SURGERY
CENTERS OF NEW JERSEY**

CLIFTON, NJ 973 473 1515 • CHESTER, NJ 908 879 7297

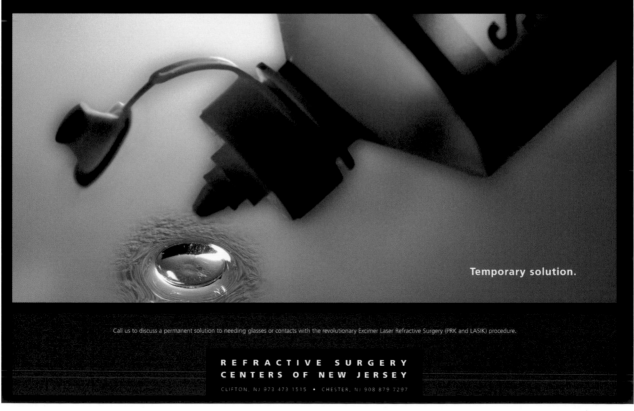

Temporary solution.

Call us to discuss a permanent solution to needing glasses or contacts with the revolutionary Excimer Laser Refractive Surgery (PRK and LASIK) procedure.

**REFRACTIVE SURGERY
CENTERS OF NEW JERSEY**

CLIFTON, NJ 973 473 1515 • CHESTER, NJ 908 879 7297

local real estate, globally

commercial real estate in over 250 locations worldwide   www.colliers.com

local real estate, globally

commercial real estate in over 250 locations worldwide   www.colliers.com

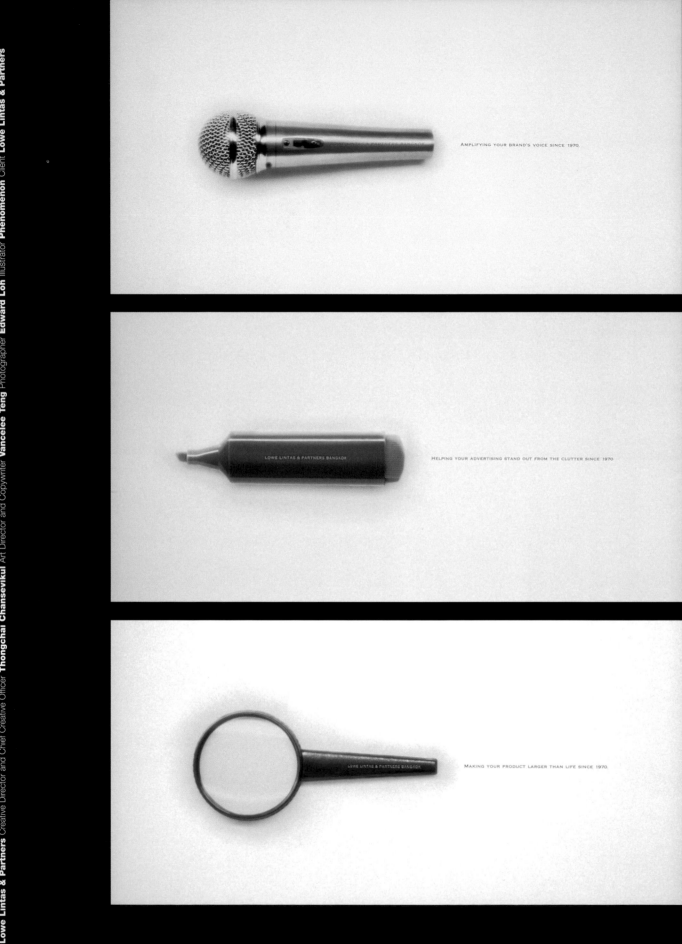

AMPLIFYING YOUR BRAND'S VOICE SINCE 1970.

LOWE LINTAS & PARTNERS BANGKOK

HELPING YOUR ADVERTISING STAND OUT FROM THE CLUTTER SINCE 1970.

LOWE LINTAS & PARTNERS BANGKOK

MAKING YOUR PRODUCT LARGER THAN LIFE SINCE 1970.

FRÖHLING Werbeagentur GmbH
www.froehling.de

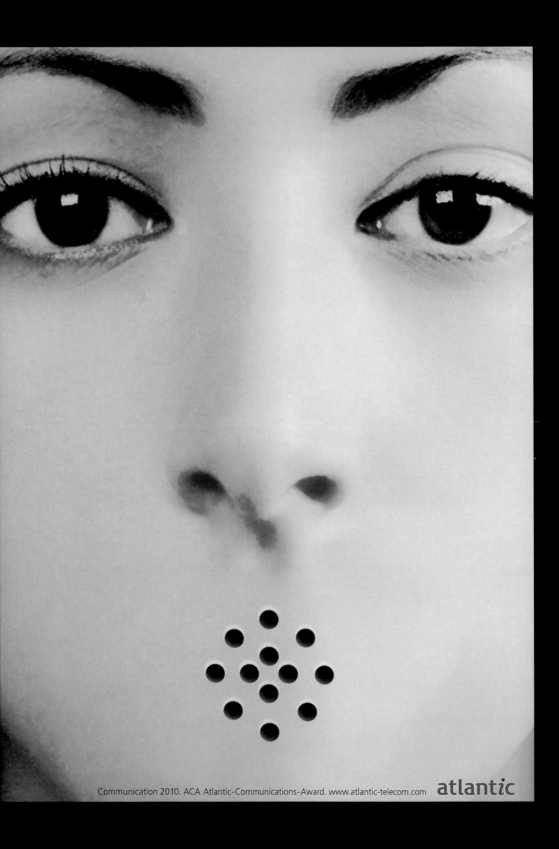

Communication 2010. ACA Atlantic-Communications-Award. www.atlantic-telecom.com

atlantic

Jan Schmodde Art Director Holger Wiesenfarth Photographer Manu Agah Copywriter Holger Senft Account Supervisors Torsten Waack and Daniele Iezz Client Atlantic Telecom

Big ideas.

Big shoes.

The world's most interesting copywriter.

Presentation skills?

Yes.

The world's most interesting copywriter.

Gumbo Creative Director Tim Heckman Art Director Mike Frey Photographer Bill Thompson Copywriter Tim Heckman

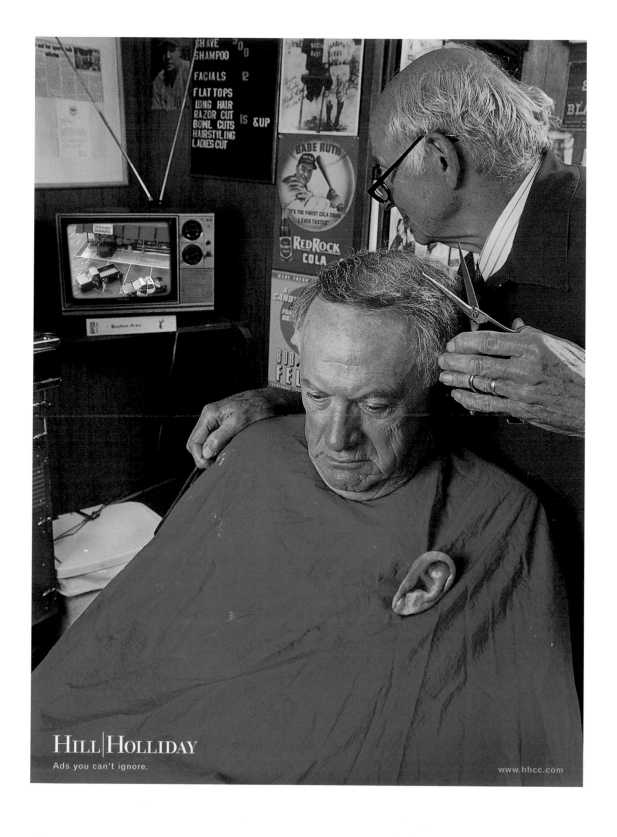

HILL|HOLLIDAY

Ads you can't ignore.

www.hhcc.com

The average grocery store
carries 16,875 brands.
Why do you recognize
this one?

Advertising. The way great brands get to be great brands.™

The secret formula, revealed.

Advertising. The way great brands get to be great brands.

GmbH Creative Directors T. Hobein and M. Leidenheimer Art Director Elke Kuhn Photographer Ingo Bach Copywriter Wiebke Kistenbruegger Client Suedwest Presse Online Dienste GmbH

www.animal-peace.org

Agency **Publicis Werbeagentur GmbH** Creative Directors **M. Boebel** and **H. Schmitt** Art Director **Marcus Luzius** Photographer **Peter Duettmann** Copywriter **Andreas Sturm** Client **Animal Peace**

Public Services 194, 195

Feuerwehr
sucht Freiwillige
069-657670

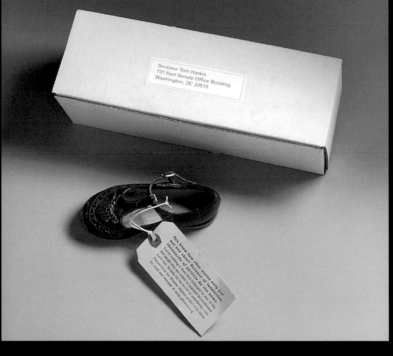

(this page) Agency **Euro RSCG Talham** Creative Director and Copywriter **Jim Schmidt** Art Director **Jeff Dechausse** Client **Physicians for Human Rights**

Public Services 196,197

I BEG YOUR PARDON DAVID. I COULDN'T PUT A BENEFIT IN THIS HEADLINE.

Agency SSC&B Lintas Creative Director Mahendra Bhagat Art Directors Shezar Hebbale and Manoj Jacob Copywriter Mallikarjun Katakol Photographer Manoj Jacob Client SSC&B Lintas

IRRESPECTIVE
CIGARETTE LENGTH : 66 mm
10

OF THE
•FILTER• 20 CIGARETTES

Brand
FILTER KINGS 20 CIGARETTES

YOU SMOKE
TOBACCO GROUP

YOU PAY ★

THE SAME 10 CIGARETTES

PRICE
123033

Agency **SSC&B Lintas** Creative Director **Mahendra Bhagat** Art Directors **Devesh Desai** and **Shekar Hebbale** Photographer **Mallikarjun Katakol** Copywriter **Manoj Jacob** Client **IndiaCares.com**

ABSOLUTE KILLER.

IT'S TRUE, LIKE MOST ALCOHOL ADVERTISING TELLS YOU, YOU ARE A CHANGED MAN AFTER DRINKING (ESPECIALLY IF YOU'VE HAD MORE THAN A FEW).
JUST TAKE YOUR PICK FROM WIFE-BEATER, RAPIST, CHILD-ABUSER, HOMICIDAL MANIAC...

ALCOHOL CHANGES YOU. A LOT MORE THAN YOU THINK.

Give dad an expensive belt.

IT'S TRUE, LIKE MOST ALCOHOL ADVERTISING TELLS YOU, YOU ARE
A CHANGED MAN AFTER DRINKING (ESPECIALLY IF YOU'VE HAD MORE THAN A FEW),
JUST TAKE YOUR PICK FROM WIFE-BEATER, RAPIST, CHILD-ABUSER, HOMICIDAL MANIAC...
ALCOHOL CHANGES YOU. A LOT MORE THAN YOU THINK.

Only buy cosmetics which have not been tested on animals. NOAH People for Animals. www.noah.de

NOAH
People for animals

Agency **Jung von Matt Werbeagentur GmbH** Creative Directors **Goetz Ulmer** and **Thorn Wildberger** Art Directors **Christian Reimer** and **Corinna Falusi** Copywriter **Christina Coates** Client **Noah Menschen Fuer Tiere eV** Public Services 200, 201

PROTECT YOURSELF FROM AIDS. USE A CONDOM.

D'Arcy/Beijing Creative Directors Eddie Wong and Tina Chen Art Director and Copywriter Eddie Wong Photographer Ricky So Illustrator Zou Yong Production Zheng Peng Client Mediastar

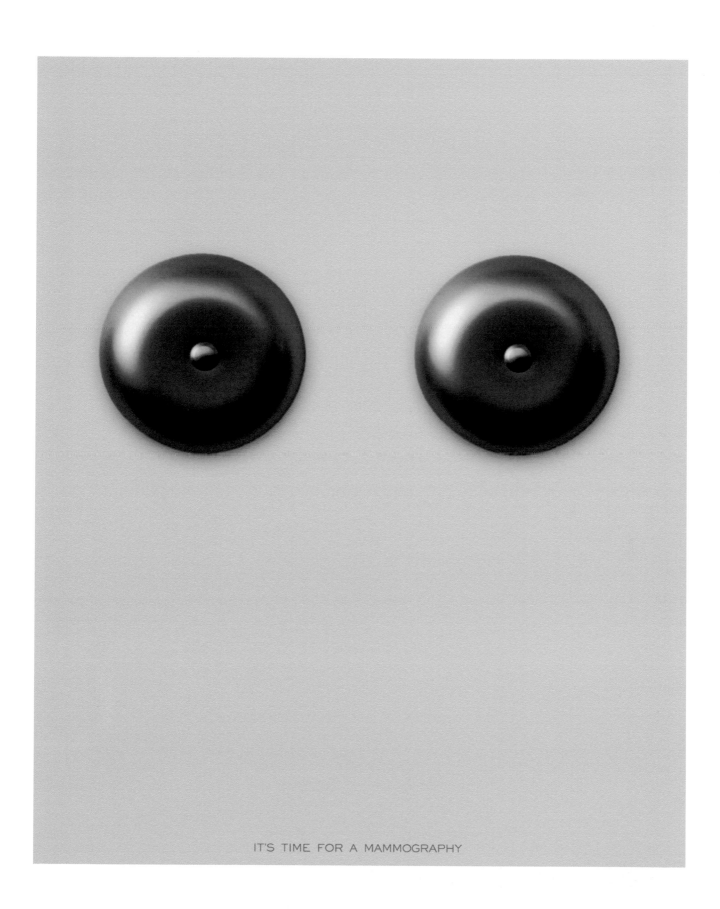

IT'S TIME FOR A MAMMOGRAPHY

Agency **Wing Latino Group** Creative Director **Osvaldo Vázquez** Art Director **Félix Castro** Designer **Anabelle Barranco** Photographer **X-Films** Copywriter **Anabelle Barranco**

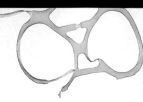

How's your day going? Has your wife or husband told you that they can't stand living with you any more? No? Somebody else's has. Did someone you love die? Have you been declared bankrupt, made redundant or been fired? Somebody has. Did you kill someone in a car accident? Maybe you were raped? Have you lost your savings on a bad investment? Somebody has. Whatever shit could happen to you today, hopefully you would be able to find a way to deal with it. Somebody won't. It will completely shatter their life. It will destroy them mentally, bit, by bit, by bit. They'll stop caring about themselves or other people, their job, mortgage payments. The worse it gets, the worse it gets. Other people, even their relatives, will all eventually give up on them. And while they're gradually losing everything, including their home, there's a fifty fifty chance that they will become an alcoholic. They'll despise themselves for what they have become. And suicide will seem the only way out. The Big Issue Foundation's a better one. It offers a chance to start again. We believe that the most effective kind of help is self-help. Selling The Big Issue magazine is not only good for the pocket, it's also good for the soul. Money that you've earned will tend to be valued more than any handout. The vendors discover that we offer support for addictions and mental illness. Job training and advice is there for those who want it. And we do whatever we can to find accommodation. The Big Issue Foundation exists because we believe that the homeless all have the potential to change their lives.

How does a normal, well-balanced member of society end up a suicidal, homeless drunk? And vice versa.

You're freezing your arse off in some doorway every night, you've got no job, no money, and sod all chance of any of it changing. You haven't got any answers but someone's got heroin. There's always someone who's got heroin. Risks? You haven't got anything to lose, remember. So you get off your face and you feel great. You don't have to think when you're wasted. It's a holiday for your brain. But it's only a short trip. It wears off and your life is still crap. If anything, it seems worse. But at least you've got something to look forward to now. The more you use it, the harder it gets to find the money for it, the more you value it, the more you want it, the harder it is to find the money that you owe for it, the more you need it, the harder it is to think about anything else. Alcohol's kind of the same. Give it up? Oh yeah, right. Why? Just because some dickhead in a duffel coat who's read a couple of Irvine Welsh books is telling you that they understand? Words are cheap. Nothing else is. Selling The Big Issue magazine is a way to earn a bit of cash. No strings. No self-righteousness. No law against it. When the vendors come to collect their magazines each week, they get to know about The Big Issue Foundation, that we offer support to help break addictions. We also offer help with mental illnesses, advice and training for jobs, and, of course, assistance with accommodation. It's there if they want it. But there's absolutely no pressure to take it. And that's why hundreds do, every year. The Foundation exists because we believe that homeless people all have the potential to change their lives. Think about it.

How can you heroin sort your life heroin out when the heroin only thing heroin you heroin can heroin think heroin about heroin is heroin?

Cream of tomato, mushroom or even spicy lentil, with or without croutons, is unlikely to have ever satisfied the obsessive cravings of your average crack addict. If mulligatawny is a more effective way of blocking out the abject misery of someone's particular existence than a can or two of super strength lager, then it would probably be illegal by now, or at least a lot more expensive than it is. And if leek and potato really is so comforting that it's ever given a whole new reason to carry on living to the most clinically depressed, then it's news to us. Not that we'd suggest for a moment that anyone should stop giving free soup to homeless people. They're glad of it. Anything is better than nothing. But other people's consciences can be all too easily satisfied by the knowledge that the homeless can always queue up for their nightly broth. They won't starve to death so that's enough is it? We, The Big Issue Foundation don't think so. People become homeless for any number of different reasons. Things go wrong at some point in their lives. Then they remain homeless for the simple reason that they come to accept their predicament, because they don't know how they can change it. Apart, that is, from those who start selling The Big Issue magazine. Earning money starts to rebuild their self-esteem. And when the vendors turn up to collect their magazines, they discover that we offer help with most of the root causes of homelessness: mental illness, various addictions and long-term unemployment. The Big Issue Foundation exists because we believe that every homeless person has the potential to change their life.

Drug addict? Alcoholic? Suicidal?
Apparently, what you need is a nice cup of hot soup.

(is page) Agency TBWA/London Creative Director Trevor Beattie Art Director and Photographer Paul Belford Copywriter Nigel Roberts Client The Big Issue Foundation

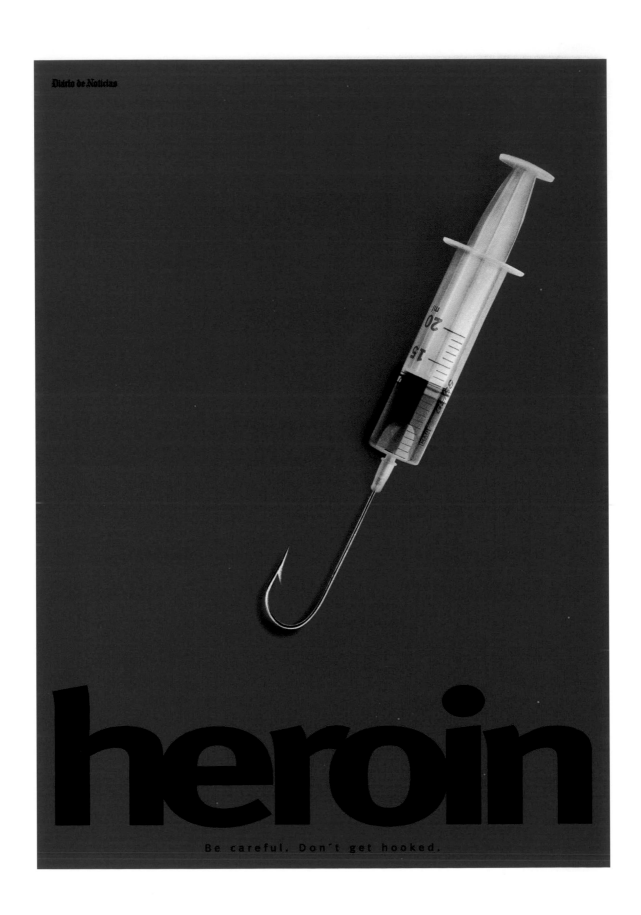

heroin

Be careful. Don't get hooked.

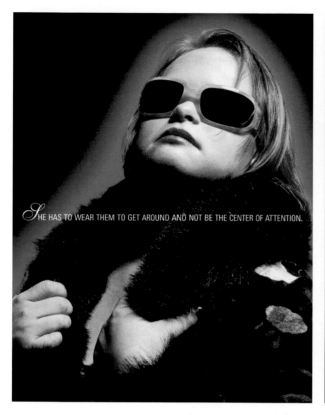

SHE HAS TO WEAR THEM TO GET AROUND AND NOT BE THE CENTER OF ATTENTION.

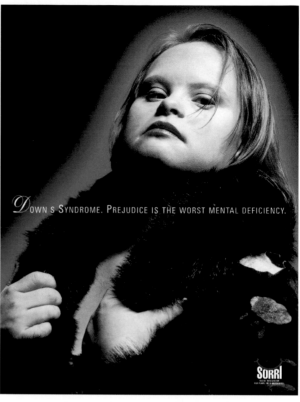

DOWN'S SYNDROME. PREJUDICE IS THE WORST MENTAL DEFICIENCY.

DON'T VOTE.
THINGS ARE PERFECT JUST THE WAY THEY ARE.

DON'T VOTE.
THINGS ARE PERFECT JUST THE WAY THEY ARE.

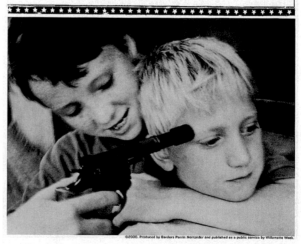

Diário de Notícias

Vasco Pulido Valente in the DN. If you find out a compliment in any of his articles, the errata will be issued the day after.

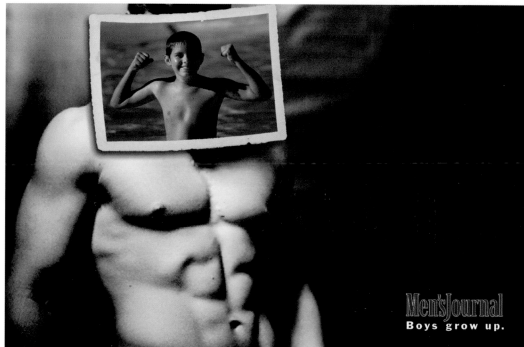

(this page) Agency **GSD&M** Creative Director, Art Director and Copywriter **Tom Gilmore** Producer **Kelly Grant** Client **Men's Journal** Publishing 208, 209

Nobody loves football more than Brazilians.

Nobody loves football more than Brazilians.

Nobody loves football more than Brazilians.

(this page) Agency **Young & Rubicam Brasil** Creative Directors **Tião Bernardi, J.R. D'Elboux** and **Rita Corradi** Art Director **Pedro Pletitsh** Photographer **Ale Ermel** Copywriter **Marcelo Sato** Client **Editora Abril** Publishing 210,211

ABSOLUT TIMES.

settebello

italian food indian style

seefeldstrasse 129, 8008 zürich

Agency **Jung von Matt/Limmat AG** Creative Director **David Honegger** Art Director **Felix Dammann** Photographer **Jonathan Heyer** Copywriter **Dominik Imseng** Client **Settebello**

Publishing/Restaurants 212,213

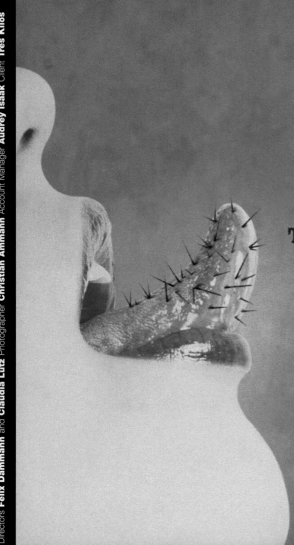

TRES KILOS · MEXICAN RESTAURANT

DUFOURSTRASSE 175 · 8008 ZÜRICH

Agency **Jung von Matt/Limmat AG** Creative Director **Daniel Meier** Art Directors **Felix Dammann** and **Claudia Lütz** Photographer **Christian Ammann** Account Manager **Audrey Isaak** Client **Tres Kilos**

(this page) Agency **Allen & Gerritsen** Creative Directors **Doug Chapman** and **Mick O'Brien** Art Director **Brian Bernier** Photographer **Brian Bernier** Art Director **Craig Orsini** Copywriter **Mike Davis** Client **Thirsty Scholar**   Restaurants 214,215

Do you believe in re-incarnation?

the pine shop

Agency **Tribe** Creative Directors **John Stapleton** and **James Rosene** Art Director **John Stapleton** Copywriter **James Rosene** Client **The Pine Shop**

UNDER YOUR SKIN

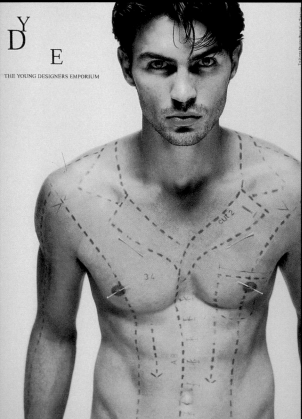

(this page) Agency **The Jupiter Drawing Room, South Africa** Creative Director **Ross Chowles** Art Director **Schalk van der Merwe** Photographer **Jillian Lochner** Copywriter **Anton Visser** Client **Y. D. E.** Retail 216, 217

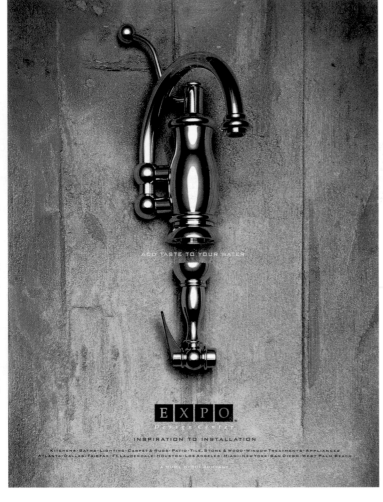

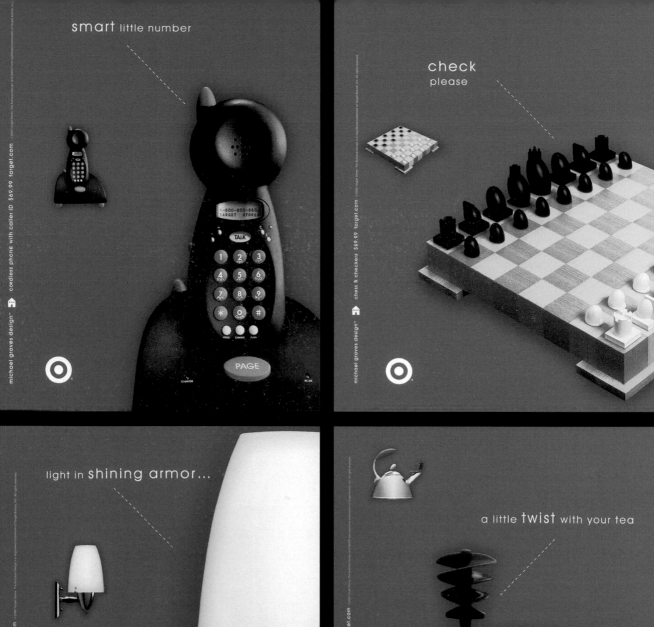

smart little number

michael graves design™ ● cordless phone with caller ID $69.99 target.com

check
please

michael graves design™ ● chess & checkers $59.99 target.com

light in shining armor...

michael graves design™ ● single wall sconce $29.99 target.com

a little twist with your tea

michael graves design™ ● spinning whistle teakettle 34.99 target.com

NAUTICAL EXTERIOR
LIGHT. AVAILABLE IN
VARIOUS METAL FINISHES
WITH A CLEAR OR
FROSTED GLASS SHADE.
UL LISTED FOR WET
LOCATIONS 100W. ONE
OF 34 EXTERIOR
SCONCES BY URBAN
ARCHAEOLOGY.

urbanARCHAEOLOGY

NEW YORK: 143 FRANKLIN STREET 212.431.4646 • 239 EAST 58TH STREET 212.371.4646
BRIDGEHAMPTON: 2231 MONTAUK HIGHWAY 631.537.1024 • WWW.URBANARCHAEOLOGY.COM

urbanARCHAEOLOGY

INSPIRED BY FRENCH
SCONCE DESIGNED IN
THE LATE 1920's.
AVAILABLE IN VARIOUS
METAL FINISHES WITH
AN ALABASTER SHADE.
UL LISTED FOR DRY
LOCATIONS 600W.
ONE OF 54 INTERIOR
SCONCES BY URBAN
ARCHAEOLOGY.

NEW YORK: 143 FRANKLIN STREET 212.431.4646 • 239 EAST 58TH STREET 212.371.4646
BRIDGEHAMPTON: 2231 MONTAUK HIGHWAY 631.537.1024 • WWW.URBANARCHAEOLOGY.COM

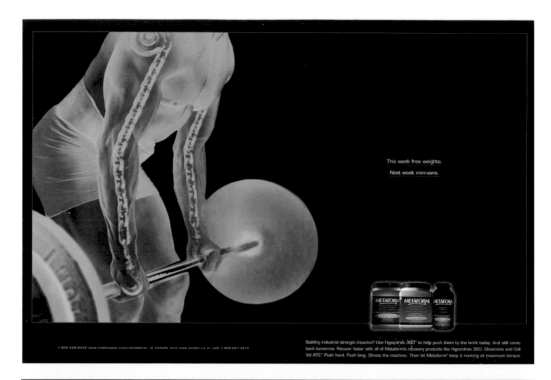

This week free weights.

Next week mini-vans.

Building industrial strength muscles? Use Hyperdrive 380™ to help push them to the brink today. And still come back tomorrow. Recover faster with all of Metaform's recovery products like Hyperdrive 380, Glutamine and Cell Vol ATS™. Push hard. Push long. Stress the machine. Then let Metaform® keep it running at maximum torque.

1-800-439-8048 www.realmuscle.com/metaform. In Canada visit www.weider.ca or call 1-800-667-4815.

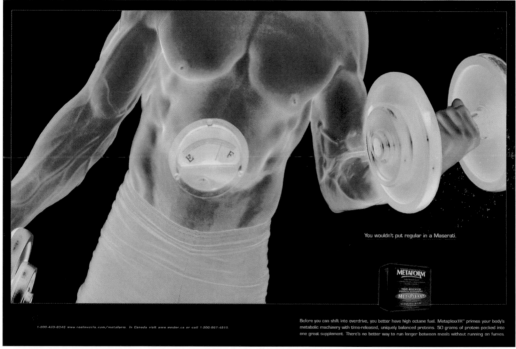

You wouldn't put regular in a Maserati.

Before you can shift into overdrive, you better have high octane fuel. MetaplexxTR™ primes your body's metabolic machinery with time-released, uniquely balanced proteins. 50 grams of protein packed into one great supplement. There's no better way to run longer between meals without running on fumes.

1-800-439-8048 www.realmuscle.com/metaform. In Canada visit www.weider.ca or call 1-800-667-4815.

The only time to quit is when they turn out the lights.

Maybe Androstenedione won't help you see in the dark. But it will help you vault over that plateau you hit. Enhance performance and break through with the Metaform® pre-workout supplements: Androstenedione and Metacuts™. They'll help you remove the word "quit" from your vocabulary.

1-800-439-8048 www.realmuscle.com/metaform. In Canada visit www.weider.ca or call 1-800-667-4815.

Agency Sasquatch Advertising Creative Directors Tim Parker and Greg Eiden Art Director Ted Pate Photographer Bob Waldman Copywriters Greg Eiden, Jason Barnes and Gary Fulkerson Client Weider   Retail/Sports 220,221

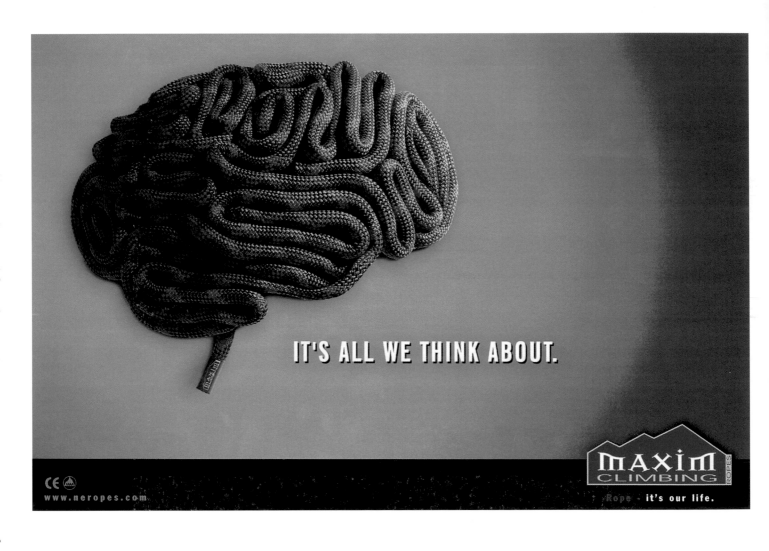

IT'S ALL WE THINK ABOUT.

www.neropes.com

MAXIM
CLIMBING ROPES

Rope · it's our life.

for tickets www.bostonbulldogs.com

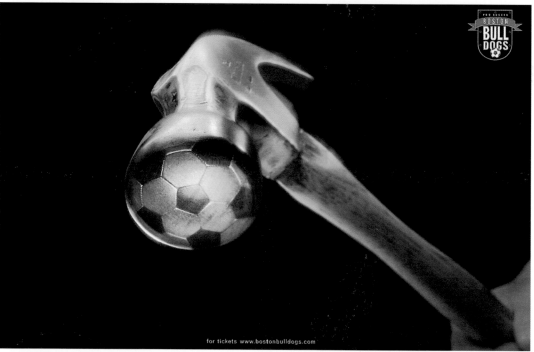

for tickets www.bostonbulldogs.com

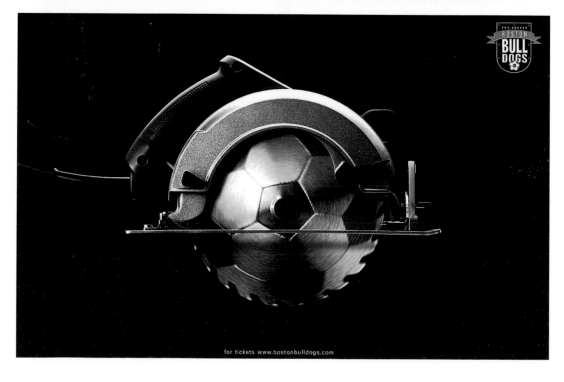

for tickets www.bostonbulldogs.com

(this page) Agency **Hill Holliday** Art Director and Designer **Don Miller** Photographer **Eric Gronlund** Copywriter **Eivind Ueland** Client **Boston Bulldogs Professional Soccer**

The Ascent with Stealth C4® rubber　909-798-4222　www.fiveten.com

The Hueco with Stealth C4® rubber　909-798-4222　www.fiveten.com

The Ascent with Stealth C4® rubber　909-798-4222　www.fiveten.com

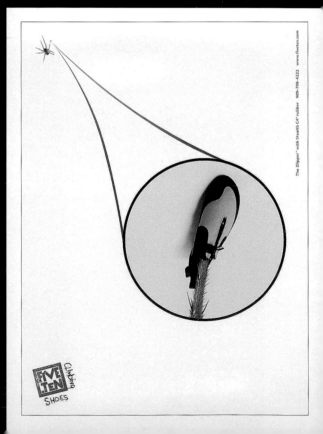

The Zipper™ with Stealth C4® rubber　909-798-4222　www.fiveten.com

Is it a plane or is it a rocket? No, it's Jesus Christ.

KILLER LOOP®

2.5.00

Remember to ski and snowboard responsibly. www.boeriusa.com

boeri
it's your head

Remember to ski and snowboard responsibly. www.boeriusa.com

boeri
it's your head

Remember to ski and snowboard responsibly. www.boeriusa.com

boeri
it's your head

(this page) Agency **Mullen** Creative Directors **Michael Ancevil, Edward Bocnes** and **Stephen Mietelski** Art Director **Mark Rich** Photographer **Craig Orsini** Copywriter **Stephen Mietelski** Client **Boeri**

pure racing

Rimanere incollati alla neve può sembrare un controsenso. Chi lo fa a più di 120 km orari conosce i vantaggi dell'abbinamento scarponi Dobermann e sci K 0.0 GS progettati per offrire il massimo controllo ad alte velocità. Gli scarponi da

gara Dobermann interamente costruiti in polietere nero e dotati del sistema di fissaggio asimmetrico Dual Axis consentono una maggior pressione interna sullo

sci in curva. Gli sci K 0.0 GS con guscio in titanio offrono la massima stabilità permettendo traiettorie precise anche su piste ripide e ghiacciate. I nuovi attacchi N2 S offrono un fissaggio preciso e proporzionato alle caratteristiche

tecniche e morfologiche dello sciatore. Per andare più veloci bisogna partire più in alto possibile. Pure technology for pure skiing.

NORDICA.

Sci K 0.0 GS - Scarpone Dobermann - Attacco N2 S

---

pure adrenaline

A volte finire fuori pista è una scelta. Per chi lo fa con passione abbiamo creato Wave Line, scarponi e sci freeride concepiti per divertirsi in condizioni estreme. La tecnologia Exopower II e le

leve Twintech in alluminio con regolazione micrometrica migliorano la trasmissione e il comfort dello scarpone W 9.1. La struttura Sandwich Ti dello sci W 9.1 F abbina

la flessibilità del nucleo alla resistenza e alla leggerezza del rivestimento in titanio, ottenendo un rapporto ideale fra flessione e rigidità torsionale. I nuovi attacchi N2 S offrono un fissaggio preciso e

proporzionato alle caratteristiche tecniche e morfologiche dello sciatore. Rischiare diventa quasi troppo facile. Pure technology for pure skiing.

NORDICA.

Sci W 9.1 F - Scarpone W 9.1 - Attacco N2 S

---

pure performance

Una pista dietro l'altra. Ore e ore sugli sci a ricercare la perfezione. È la parte più dura è stare seduti in funivia. Per gli imperterriti perfezionisti dello stile, Nordica ha sviluppato K line, scarponi e sci ideati per garantire la curva

ideale a tutte le velocità. Gli scarponi K 9.1, con leve Twintech in alluminio a regolazione micro-metrica, consentono la massima trasmissione dell'energia grazie al

design Exopower II. Gli sci K 9.1 sono costruiti con tecnologia Nordibridge e rivestiti in Titanio per distribuire la presa laterale mente e ottenere un'incisiva presa di spigolo e velocissimi cambi di direzione. I nuovi attacchi N2 S offrono un

fissaggio preciso e proporzionato alle caratteristiche tecniche e morfologiche dello sciatore. Pure technology for pure skiing.

NORDICA.

Sci K 9.1 GS - Scarpone K 9.1 - Attacco N2 S

Fingertip Control.

SuperHorn. The lightest all-round rig on the water. Easy rig. Easy ride. Easy action.

NEILPRYDE

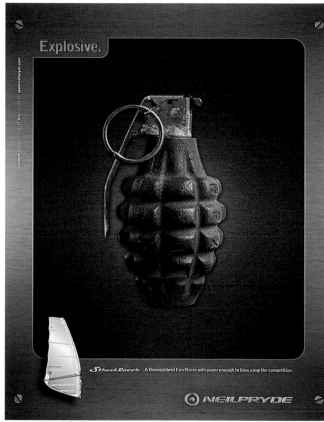

Explosive.

StreetRacer. A thoroughbred FreeRacer with power enough to blow away the competition.

NEILPRYDE

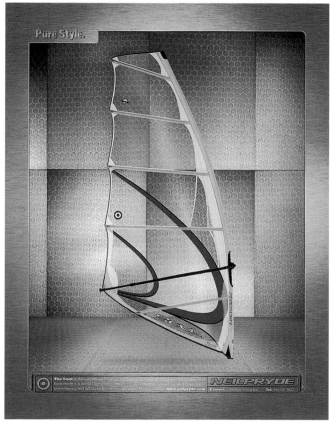

Pure Style.

The Soul is the sensational new rig from NeilPryde. Applying its unique design, the features have made it a World Cup winner.

NEILPRYDE

www.neilpryde.com   Contact: Adventure Sports Inc.   Tel: 305-591-3922

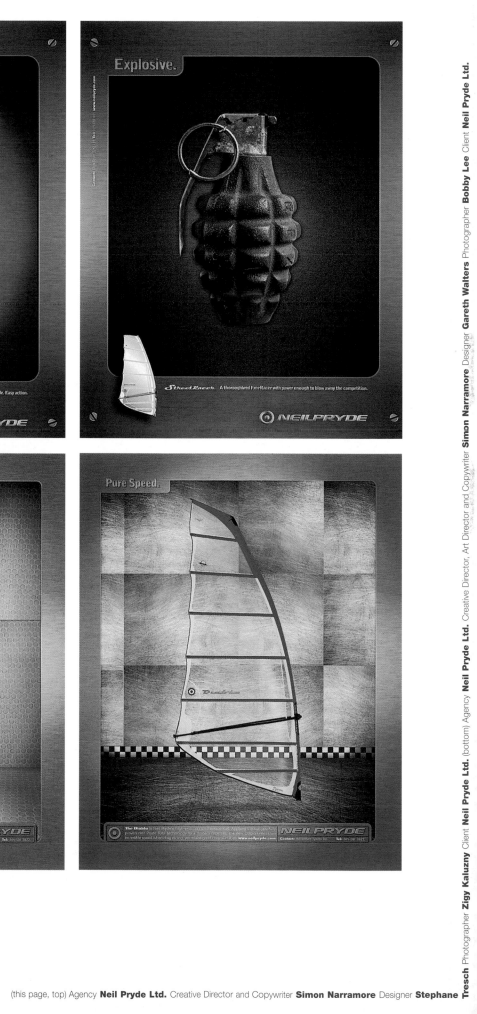

Pure Speed.

The Diablo is NeilPryde's fastest, most advanced rig. Applying its unique design, incredible speed when drag racing, yet retains great control.

NEILPRYDE

www.neilpryde.com   Contact: Adventure Sports Inc.   Tel: 305-591-3922

Sports 230, 231

Tresch Photographer **Zigy Kaluzny** Client Neil Pryde Ltd. (bottom) Agency **Neil Pryde Ltd.** Creative Director, Art Director and Copywriter **Simon Narramore** Designer **Gareth Walters** Photographer **Bobby Lee** Client Neil Pryde Ltd.

(this page, top) Agency **Neil Pryde Ltd.** Creative Director and Copywriter **Simon Narramore** Designer **Stephane**

(this page) Agency **FCB Seattle** Creative Director **Fred Hammerquist** Art Director **Andy Nordfors** Photographer **Bob Peterson** Copywriter **Cal McAllister** Client **Diadora**

Fast isn't fast enough. At these tables, recruits perform combat training drills on Diadora's Morpho. Its custom cleat configuration and touch control layer make it the world's most formidable weapon. Above, a careless plebe falls out of favor with his Italian drill instructor!— but rest easy. Discipline ensures the team's welfare. They're in **Diadora Boot Camp.**

The journey is complete. These proud recruits stand smartly before their Italian commander at final inspection. Armed with Morphos*, it's now a waiting game until the call for combat beckons* **our troops** *to the field. Please hold your tears, mothers and girlfriends. Victory is only 90 minutes away. For they are graduates of* **Diadora Boot Camp.**

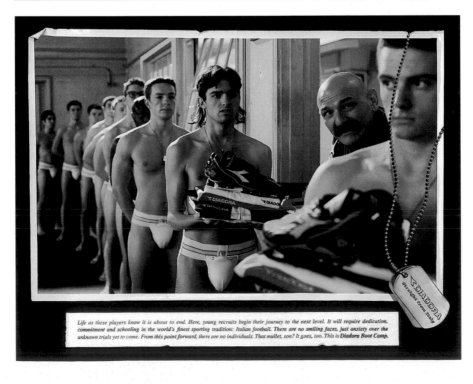

Life as these players know it is about to end. Here, young recruits begin their journey to the next level. It will require dedication, commitment and schooling in the world's finest sporting tradition: Italian football. There are no smiling faces, just anxiety over the unknown trials yet to come. From this point forward, there are no individuals. That mullet, son? It goes, too. This is **Diadora Boot Camp.**

for more detailed information on our newest mountain bikes go to cannondale.com

cannondale

©2002 cannondale corp.

for more detailed information on our newest mountain bikes go to cannondale.com

cannondale

©2002 cannondale corp.

this page) Agency **TDA Advertising & Design** Creative Director and Copywriter **Jonathan Schoenberg** Art Director **Thomas Dooley** Photographer **Brooks Freehill** Client **Cannondale**

for more detailed information on our newest mountain bikes go to cannondale.com

cannondale

©2002 cannondale corp.

The Specialized Vegas TJ.

Enjoy the view.

specialized.com

dirt jumping specific geometry   no-oval headtube   05 3-pc cranks

The Specialized Vegas TJ.

Arise.

specialized.com

dirt jumping specific geometry   no-oval headtube   48 spoke wheels

(this page) Agency **Goodby, Silverstein & Partners** Creative Directors **Jeffrey Goodby** and **Rich Silverstein** Art Director **Paul Hirsch** Illustrators **The Clayton Brothers** Copywriter **Josh Denberg** Client **Specialized**

The classic Romeo Y Julieta 1875 is back.

Let Loose for 30 minutes.

Introducing Aquarius. Like nothing you've ever tasted.

Let Loose for 30 minutes.

Introducing Aquarius. Like nothing you've ever tasted.

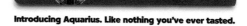

The classic Romeo y Julieta 1875 is back.

The classic Romeo y Julieta 1875 is back.

Brian Ganton, Jr. Art Director **Christopher Ganton** Copywriter **Mark Ganton** Client **BR Cigars** (bottom) Agency **WestWayne** Art Director **Jennifer Martin** Photographer **Greg Slater** Copywriter **Beth Stewart** Client **Tabacalera de España** Tobacco 236,237

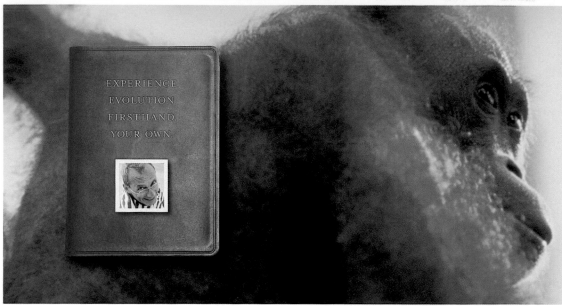

EXPERIENCE
EVOLUTION
FIRSTHAND.
YOUR OWN.

One can't venture into some of the most remote regions of the planet without returning a changed person. That is the beauty of embarking on one of our expeditions. Along the way, you will become one with magical, mystical worlds that will come face-to-face with creatures most people only read about in books. You will also come face-to-face with gourmet dinners, crisp sheets, and four-star lodging. And you might even discover that the animals you once thought exotic are almost like family.

The Highroad To The Ends Of The Earth
www.ietravel.com / 1-800-633-4734

SOMETIMES IT'S
NICE TO SPEND YOUR
SUMMER VACATION
IN A THEME PARK
CREATED BY GOD.

The most breathtaking amusement park on Earth was not created by a cartoon company. Take one of our expeditions, and along the way you and yours will become one with magical, mystical worlds that are home to some of the planet's rarest, most exotic plants and animals. Africa, Galapagos, the Amazon, and more. Consequently, you will also become one with gourmet dinners, crisp sheets, and four-star accommodations of all kinds. A lot of things grow in the wild, and your family can too.

The Highroad To The Ends Of The Earth
www.ietravel.com / 1-800-633-4734

LOOK AT IT THIS WAY. IF THE JONESES WANT TO KEEP UP WITH YOU, THEY'LL HAVE TO GO HALFWAY AROUND THE WORLD.

It'll be hard to top the awe-inspiring stories you will return with after journeying into the far reaches of the planet with us. Tales of giant lizards, monkeys of all kinds, or even sightings of rare river dolphins of the Amazon. From Africa to Belize, Galapagos to the Amazon. You'll also return with stories of the gourmet meals, courteous guides, and four-star lodgings. Sometimes it's nice to remind yourself that there are still jungles out there not made of concrete.

The Highroad To The Ends Of The Earth
www.ietravel.com / 1-800-633-4734

IF THIS WERE A THEME PARK, THE MASCOT WOULD BE CHARLES DARWIN.

Like Darwin, you too will find the Galapagos Islands a place of inspiration. Journey with us into these islands, and you will become one with some of the most exotic primates and plant life known to man. Along the way, you will also become one with gourmet dinners, crisp sheets, and four-star accommodations of all kinds. And you might even come to believe in evolution, your own that is.

VOYAGES
The Highroad To The Ends Of The Earth
www.ietravel.com / 1-800-633-4734

Photographers Pat Powell (top) Galen Rowell and Geoff Knight (bottom) Frans Lanting and Geoff Knight Illustrators David Webb and Doug Benson Copywriter Dave Smith Client International Expeditions

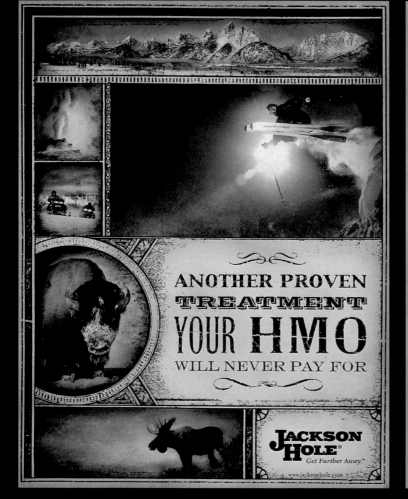

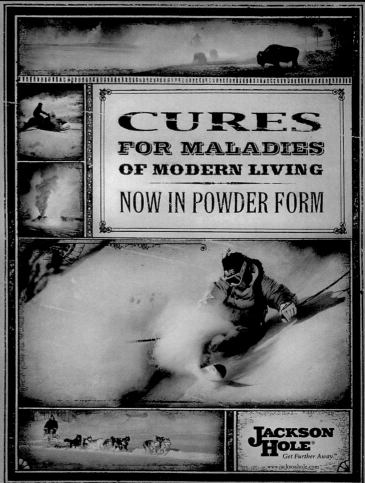

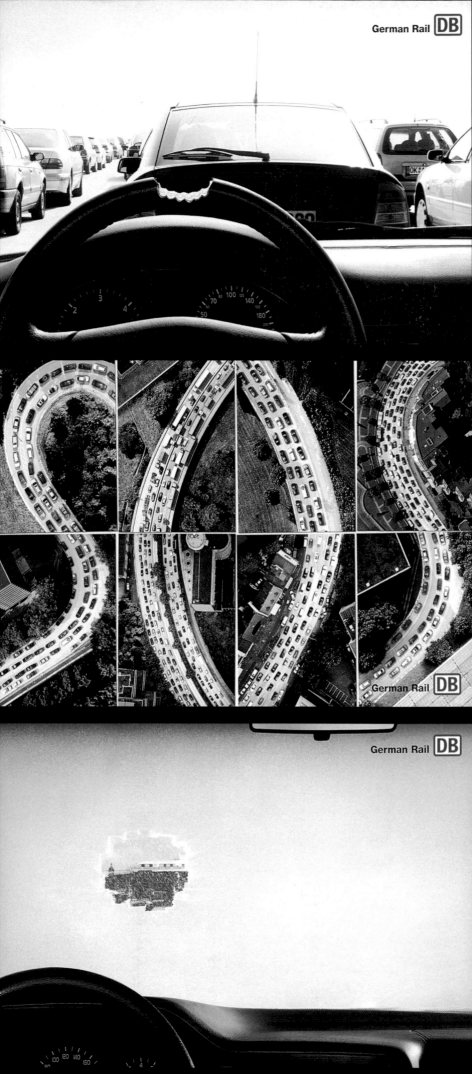

German Rail **DB**

German Rail **DB**

German Rail **DB**

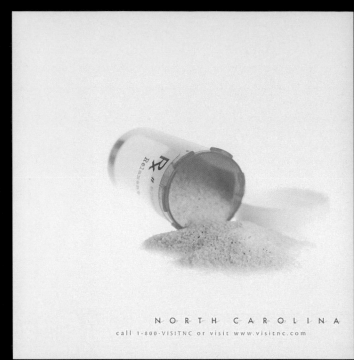

Client Curtis Smith Copywriter Pat Staub (bottom right) Steve Murray (bottom left) and Pat Staub (top) George Humphries and Pat Staub (bottom right) Steve Murray (bottom left) and Pat Staub (top) George Humphries Photographers (top) Pat Staub (top) Doug Pedersen Art Director Jim Mountjoy Creative Director Jim Mountjoy Agency Loeffler Ketchum Mountjoy

Phoenix

San Francisco

Vancouver

Pittsburgh

New York

Cape Cod

New Orleans

Miami

North Carolina

SCALE OF MILES

0   25   50   100

For Locations that can look like..Anywhere
Call..(919) 733-9900
Or Visit..www.telefilm-south.com

NORTH CAROLINA FILM COMMISSION

Agency Loeffler Ketchum Mountjoy Creative Director Jim Mountjoy Art Director Doug Pedersen Illustrator Jon Steele Copywriter Curtis Smith Client North Carolina Film Commission

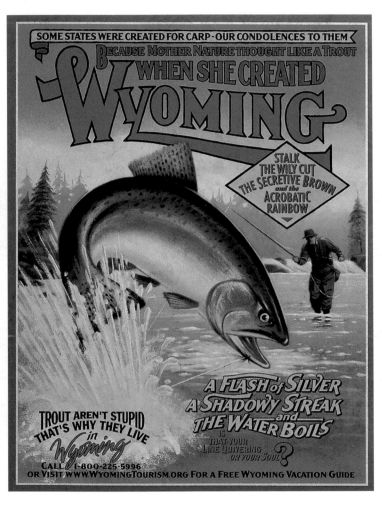

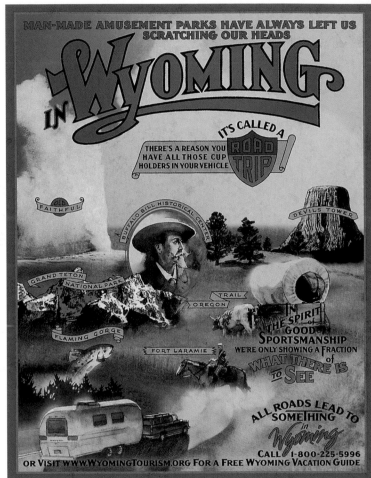

A reminder to all the teams in this month's tournament: Never underestimate the importance of getting enough rest.

COURTYARD.

The hotel designed by business travelers.

The Late Passengerassic Period

Quick yet dimwitted, *Travelerus neanderthalus* spent much of its time running through airports, trying to make up for time lost holding on the phone and waiting in lines. Fossil evidence suggests it was eventually displaced by the more advanced *Homo alaskapithicus*, who learned to use Alaska Airlines' website, alaskaair.com, to book tickets, purchase vacation packages and even check in online.

Driven to extinction by hold music?

Was alaskaair.com the result of a more advanced species? Or was the more advanced species a result of alaskaair.com?

The Line Waiting Ritual

Recently unearthed evidence suggests a strange pattern of pre-flight behavior among our air traveling ancestors: In search of boarding passes, large tribes would gather and stand single file for long periods of time. Eventually, modern travelers would learn to use simple tools like the Alaska Airlines Instant Travel Machine to check themselves in, select their seats, receive their boarding passes, even check their own baggage. All without waiting in long lines.

These fossilized footprints indicate that the herding instinct was strong among primitive passengers

Self check-in marked the arrival of a new species – Boardus instantaneous

CreativeDirectorsArtDirectorsDesigners

CreativeDirectorsArtDirectorsDesigners

PhotographersIllustrators

Copywriters

Agencies Design Firms

Clients

Clients

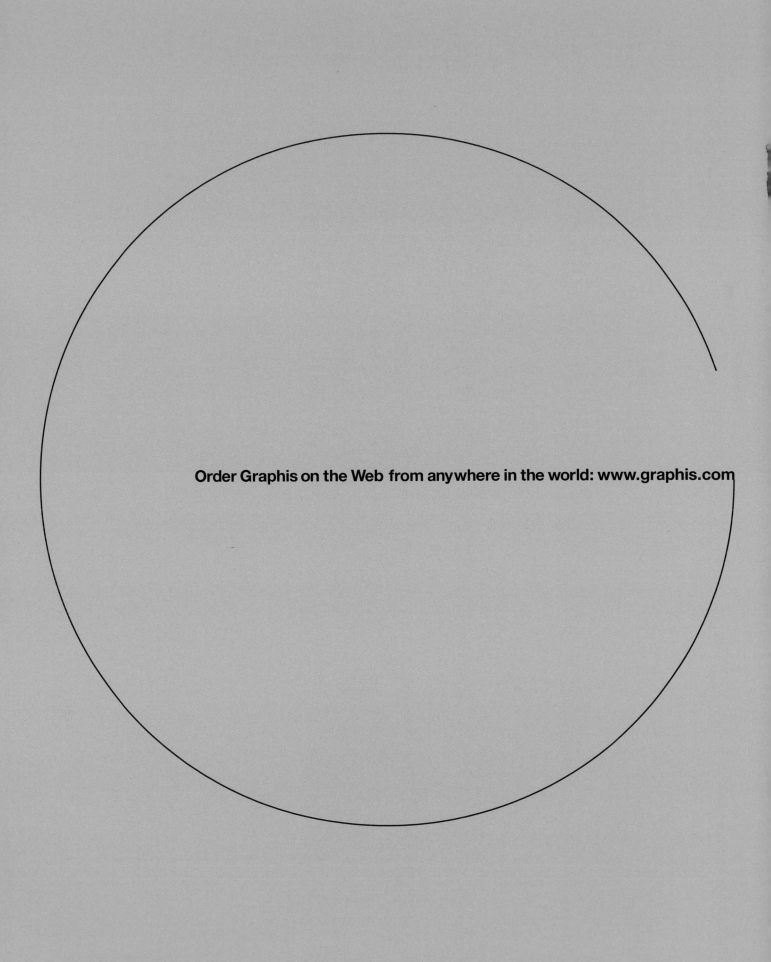

Order Graphis on the Web from anywhere in the world: www.graphis.com